# SCHOONER

BELIEVE ME, MY YOUNG FRIEND,
THERE IS NOTHING — ABSOLUTELY
NOTHING — HALF SO MUCH WORTH
DOING AS SIMPLY MESSING ABOUT
IN BOATS...

KENNETH GRAHAM,
WIND IN THE WILLOWS

*For Joe,*
*Despite everything.*
*Fair winds and following seas!*

# SCHOONER

## Building a wooden boat on Martha's Vineyard

*By* Tom Dunlop
*Photographs by* Alison Shaw

*A lovely friend —*
*Jan Pogue*

Tom Dunlop

Vineyard Stories, Edgartown, Massachusetts

# NUTS AND BOLTS...

With thanks to the Martha's Vineyard Museum for historical drawings on pages 8 and 10.
Photo page 21 courtesy of the William J. Clinton Presidential Library.
Photos pages 27, 30, and 86 courtesy of Mark Alan Lovewell, with sincere thanks. Copyright ©Mark Alan Lovewell.
Photos pages 29, 154, 155 courtesy of Louisa Gould. Copyright ©Louisa Gould.
Photo page 31 courtesy of *Martha's Vineyard Times*. Republished with permission.
Photo page 64 courtesy of John Blanding, Globe staff. Copyright ©1990, Globe Newspaper Company. Republished with permission.
Photo page 65 courtesy of Donna T. Ruhlman. Copyright ©Donna T. Ruhlman.
Photos pages 138, 150 courtesy of Tim Wright. Copyright ©Tim Wright.
Photos pages 153, 155 courtesy of Benjamin Mendlowitz. Copyright ©Benjamin Mendlowitz.
Photo page 155 courtesy of Brian Dowley. Copyright ©Brian Dowley.

Published by Vineyard Stories
RR 1, Box 65-B9
Edgartown, MA 02539
508 221 2338
www.vineyardstories.com

Library of Congress Number: 2010920192
ISBN 978-0-615-34267-2

Editor: Jan Pogue, Vineyard Stories
Designer: Sue Dawson

With grateful appreciation to Nat Benjamin and Ross Gannon.

Printed in China

This book is dedicated to John Walter
1947–2008

*From his wife and children.*

THE ISLAND

Wave of sorrow do not drown me now.
I see the Island still ahead somehow.
I see the Island and its sands are fair
Wave of sorrow take me there.

*Langston Hughes*

# contents

8   Foreword
    *Matthew Stackpole*

10   Her First Voyage

14   CHAPTER 1: Boatyard

32   CHAPTER 2: Lofting

48   CHAPTER 3: Keel

60   CHAPTER 4: Framing

76   CHAPTER 5: Planking

92   CHAPTER 6: Interior

102   CHAPTER 7: An Unwelcome Respite

104   CHAPTER 8: Deck

120   CHAPTER 9: Aloft

134   CHAPTER 10: Launch

150   At Sea

152   Afterword
      *Nat Benjamin*

154   30 Years of Boats

156   Glossary

158   Acknowledgments and Thanks

159   Sources

# foreword

"Ships are the closest things to dreams that hands have ever made."

ROBERT N. ROSE, *poet and sailor*

In the late 1800s, Vineyard Haven Harbor would often have more than a hundred big schooners anchored between the East and West Chops, waiting for the tide to go fair for them.

This is a fine book about the design and building of a beautiful new wooden schooner. But it is more than that. It's a story about dreams, tradition, initiative, personal values, perseverance, a place, and a community.

Given their shared love of the sea, it isn't surprising that Nat Benjamin and Ross Gannon were both drawn to the Vineyard in the early 1970s. What is perhaps surprising is that they should ultimately choose to begin a business focused on what many would have then argued was a vestigial material and a dying craft. After all, fiberglass was the miracle material of the future, and wood and the skills of wooden boatbuilding were relics of the past. But Vineyard Haven, with both a strong history of wooden boatbuilding and an intriguing array of wooden vessels, most dramatically represented by the square topsail schooner *Shenandoah* – the physical and symbolic centerpiece of the harbor – had attracted and inspired them both.

The creation of Gannon and Benjamin thirty years ago was welcomed by Vineyard Haven's vibrant wooden boat community, and ultimately a much larger customer base. Showing singular Island kinsmanship, the other marine enterprises in this working harbor also saw the new business not as a competitor but instead as an asset.

Nat and Ross share a passion for wooden boats and a phenomenal work ethic. A fellow sailor and good friend nicknamed the yard "The Temple of Work," as it seemed no matter what the time of day someone was always in the shop working; the name stuck.

But the two boatbuilders would be the first to say they bring different perspective and expertise to the table, a reality that is integral to their success. Gannon and Benjamin supported and nurtured the vessels and their owners with a combination of technical skills, the personal sailing experiences of Nat and Ross, an unusual openness and access to tools, and expertise for people ranging from world cruisers to young people and romantic idealists who just wanted to be a part of something special. As the yard evolved from simply wooden boat maintenance to building Nat's designs, its impact on the look of Vineyard Haven Harbor grew until today it is impossible to look at any part of the harbor without seeing examples of their work. Throughout, they have been a resource to all who share their love of "messing about in boats," to the great benefit of their island.

*Rebecca* represents a chapter in Gannon and Benjamin's story that reflects the passion, integrity, resourcefulness, generosity of thought and spirit, and ethos that make the boatyard a treasured component of Vineyard life. Nine years ago I had the privilege of speaking at *Rebecca*'s launching on that glorious day in May. As I stood on a platform beneath her bow and looked out at the hundreds of people filling every space along the vessel and railway, I was struck by what a cross section of Vineyarders were there, along with fellow sailors and wooden boat enthusiasts, some of whom had traveled from around the country and indeed the world. They had come to share in the celebration of this lovely new vessel, and I could see and literally feel a collective joy. Their presence was an affirmation not only of the beautiful new vessel about to join all her sisters, but also of the quality, character, and commitment of all the people and families that made her existence possible, and what their collective efforts contributed to the character of the Island community today.

New boat design is both a science and an art. Like composing music, all designs result from centuries of evolution of form and function. Thus, while many vessels resemble others, each new design has subtle differences which result from the designer's eye and personal experiences. I was once a guest on the forty-five-foot sloop *Liberty*, one of Nat's earliest designs, anchored in Tarpaulin Cove on Nausion Island just off the Vineyard coast. An elderly gentleman rowed by as we were enjoying our morning coffee on the deck, and without introduction inquired, "Is she an L. Frances or a Nat?" referring to two famous Herreshoff boat designers. My host replied, "No, that Nat," pointing toward the Vineyard. The gentleman immediately responded, "Oh, a Benjamin," and rowed on without further comment.

All islands are inexorably defined by the sea around them. These waters are both a barrier, and thanks to boats, a connector to all the other places water touches. How this challenge and opportunity has been and is being met is a fundamental part of Vineyard history and life, and Gannon and Benjamin will forever be credited with answering that call.

And now, enjoy your voyage aboard the beautiful *Rebecca of Vineyard Haven*, a schooner for the ages.

*Matthew Stackpole*

*Charles W. Morgan* Restoration Project, Mystic Seaport

△ On the afternoon of May 8, 2001, Matthew Stackpole, then the executive director of the Martha's Vineyard Museum, addresses the crowd attending the launch of *Rebecca of Vineyard Haven*. Stackpole is now working to help preserve America's last surviving wooden whaleship, *Charles W. Morgan*, built in 1841.

# her first voyage

DAY 1215
Early May 2001: *Rebecca* moves from boatbuilding shed to launch site.

MARTHA'S VINEYARD MUSEUM

The *Vineyard Gazette*, reporting on the launch of the largest vessel built on the Island before *Rebecca*, November 2, 1860: "A NEW VESSEL: Hon. Thomas Bradley has just launched from his shipyard at Holmes' Hole, a beautiful [brig] of 280 tons. She will be called, and very appropriately, *Island Queen*, being at once the largest and best vessel ever built on the Vineyard. . . . Her beautiful model and fine proportions do honor to her builders."

The morning she first comes into the sunlight, everyone wants to see her from the side. For three and a half years, the men and women who built this schooner have worked on her from every angle, from above and below, side to side, and end to end. In heat and cold, they've abused their knees on plywood floors, contorted their backs beneath the spread of her hull, leaned into chain saws, lathes, and planes until the muscles in their wrists tingled, arms ached, and shoulders burned. But they've never really been able to *see* her within the narrow confines of the wooden shed where she was built.

In a few moments the profile, bow-to-stern view of the schooner will finally show them how she really looks.

"First time for all of us," says Nat Benjamin, her designer and principal builder. In 1980 – thirty years ago this summer – with his partner Ross Gannon, a fellow builder and engineer, Nat founded the Gannon and Benjamin Marine Railway at the head of Vineyard Haven Harbor on the Island of Martha's Vineyard. Today Gannon and Benjamin is one of only a few full-time boatyards on either seaboard dedicated exclusively to the design, construction, repair, and maintenance of traditional wooden boats.

*Rebecca*, a two-masted schooner, is on this day in 2001 the thirty-fourth boat built by Gannon and Benjamin, and at sixty feet and 76,224 pounds by far the largest. Indeed, she will be the biggest vessel of power or sail to be launched from any harbor on the Vineyard since the election of Abraham Lincoln in 1860.

Nat stands on one side of the entrance to the boatbuilding shed, Ross on the other. It is a May morning in Vineyard Haven, hot, dry, and still. Before them, framed by what remains of the face of the building, rises the bow of *Rebecca*. The day before, her crew of builders, many of them young men in their middle twenties and some shaggy and bearded like Nat and Ross, took chain saws and crowbars to the front of the shed, tearing it away up to the second-story window so the schooner can be pulled into daylight. This will be the start of her first voyage – an eighteen-hundred-foot journey over land from the yard where she was built to the marine railway down which she will be launched into the harbor.

◁ Nat Benjamin, designer and builder of *Rebecca*, guides the schooner from her boatbuilding shed. In five days' time, *Rebecca* will be launched with speeches and Champagne before a cheering crowd of four hundred Vineyarders.

Nat first drew the lines for this schooner nearly six years earlier. Now, in the moments before *Rebecca* appears to the world, he guesses if anything is to surprise him about how she's turned out, it might be her sheer line, which defines how gracefully the hull sweeps from bow to stern. "I think we gave her more sheer back aft than I drew. That usually happens in the lofting," he says, referring to the time, just before building actually starts, when the design is redrawn, full-length, along the floor where the boat will be built. "You tend to bring the ends up a little there."

Within the shed, the schooner rests on a Brownell trailer, her hull balanced by four hydraulic and padded arms. Nat and Ross stand on either side of the tongue of the trailer; it's hooked to a truck that idles just behind them. The truck shifts into gear and the brakes release with a hiss. For those who look at their watches,

Technical specifications,
schooner *Rebecca*:

Length overall: 60 feet

Length at waterline: 45 feet

Beam: 14 feet, 8 inches

Draft: 8 feet, 6 inches

Displacement (weight):
   76,224 pounds

Sail area: 1,750 square feet

Boatbuilders tend to
measure the size of boats
by weight (or displacement)
rather than by length.
Displacement increases
exponentially as length
increases incrementally:
The largest boat built by
Gannon and Benjamin
before *Rebecca* – the
schooner *Lana and Harley*,
launched in 1988 – measures
forty-four feet on deck and
displaces 30,000 pounds.
*Rebecca* will measure sixty
feet on deck and displace
more than 76,000 pounds.

the journey begins at twenty minutes past nine, Thursday, May 3, 2001. Nat and Ross check the clearance on either side – it's tight.

The truck and trailer inch forward, revealing the bow of the boat, with the uppermost point edging its way just below where the second-story window was. The varnish on the rail cap of the bow catches the morning sun and gleams. The hull is faultlessly white, the waterline a narrow belt of bright red bottom paint. Below this, the planking in the bottom of the hull is orange, coated with a wood primer called red lead.

It is by looking at the bottom that spectators – and there are perhaps a hundred of them this morning: clerks who've come out from their nearby shops, Islanders who've followed the construction for more than three years, friends and family of the builders, those who've read the papers and know this is moving day for a historic boat – can tell that this is a vessel built of wood, an old-fashioned method in a latest-thing age of fiberglass and aluminum. Even if they know nothing of boats, they can see, at a glance, what traditional boatbuilders mean when they talk about the enduring virtues of simplicity and strength in "plank-on-frame" construction.

In a minute and a half, the whole of *Rebecca*'s hull lies before the crowd, longer than any visitor who'd seen her inside the shed could ever have imagined. Ross throws his arms around Nat. For a few moments, they say nothing. Then, with the crew and her owners, Pamela and Brian Malcolm of Traquair, Scotland, they walk a hundred feet across the dusty lot, climb the back stairs to a row of shops, and take in the profile view. The schooner, which filled the shed so imposingly for so long, is surprisingly sleek, almost rakish. There is indeed a slight but noticeable rise in the sheer line at the stern, as Nat predicted.

"She does look great," says Ross, smiling, "but that's not a surprise." In *Rebecca*'s lines and layout, he sees the influences of several generations of great American yacht designers: "Alden, Rhodes, Burgess, a little Herreshoff mixed in there. Pick up any old boat book and page through it and you'll see similar boats."

*Rebecca* has already experienced more history in her shed than many boats know in a lifetime on the water. In the past three and a half years, while still under construction, the schooner project sailed through a federal bankruptcy court once, endured two work stoppages lasting most of the previous two calendar years, known two sets of owners, and earned a reputation in Vineyard Haven as a boat that knows how to get herself out of trouble, even without moving an inch. Her trip to the launch site today, despite all the financial and legal travails, proves it.

"A boat has its own destiny," Nat likes to say. The Malcolms – who bought *Rebecca* at the bankruptcy auction six months earlier and have directed and financed the end of the work – agree: "She's an ambassador for wooden boats at a time when there are hardly any new ones built," says Pamela. "She'll have her own uniqueness, because no piece of wood is fashioned in exactly the same way."

The truck pulls *Rebecca* down a narrow lane between the shops and a split-rail fence, across a parking lot, and up to Beach Road. Police stop traffic in both directions; the schooner is too large for cars to pass as she backs down to the launching site on Vineyard Haven Harbor. As she makes the turn and begins to roll stern-first down Beach Road, a piper, Tony Peak of Tisbury, plays Scottish airs: "Road to the Isles," "Skye Boat Song," and "Highland Laddie." The crowd has grown into a parade, flanking the hull on either side as she moves slowly in reverse toward the launching site. High up on deck, her crew of young builders – in one sense her first passengers – uses oars and pieces of scrap lumber to lift telephone and power lines over *Rebecca*'s deckhouses as the schooner passes beneath them.

The left-hand turn onto the railway – an iron track on which large boats are rolled down to a harbor and launched – is sharp. Boat storage sheds loom over the road; for nearly ten minutes, the truck edges back and forth through the turn, the cab finally clearing the front of the nearest shed by less than a foot. *Rebecca* and her trailer are loaded onto the track and locked into place about forty feet short of the water's edge. The schooner rests on the same railway from which the brig *Island Queen*, the largest sailing vessel ever built on the Vineyard, may have been launched just before Lincoln's election in 1860. Awaiting *Rebecca* in Vineyard Haven Harbor is the most concentrated collection of recreational wooden boats in any harbor on either coast, many of them designed and built and many more restored or maintained by the Gannon and Benjamin Marine Railway.

In five days' time, it will be *Rebecca*'s turn to join them.

In the nine years that follow her launch, *Rebecca* will sail up and down the eastern seaboard between the Caribbean and Maine twice; across the Atlantic once; cruise the Mediterranean from Gibraltar to the west coast of Italy and back; and compete in six classic yacht regattas in the Caribbean, United Kingdom, and Mediterranean, winning two. Now, in 2010, *Rebecca* begins her tenth year on the water as Nat Benjamin and Ross Gannon celebrate their thirtieth year of building wooden boats in the most simple, proven, and beautiful way imaginable: the traditional way.

▽ Nat's early rendering of *Rebecca*, known as the sail plan, shows her hull above the waterline and keel below, her taller mainmast and shorter foremast, and four principal sails.

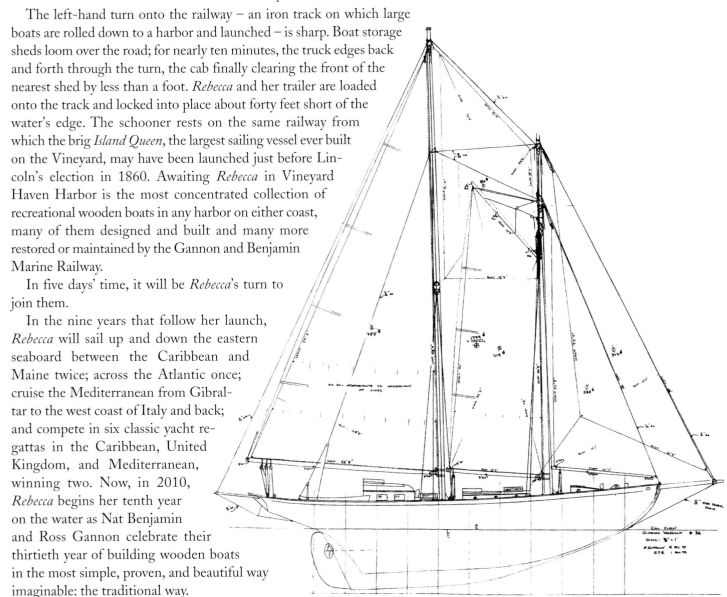

boatyard

The main boatbuilding shed of the Gannon and Benjamin Marine Railway on Vineyard Haven Harbor. Boats built or repaired under this open-air shed are loaded onto one of two cradles, foreground, and launched down a track into the harbor.

They each came to Martha's Vineyard with long experiences of – and a profound respect for – things built the old-fashioned way.

In the late spring of 1974, Ross Gannon, a trained engineer who moved to Martha's Vineyard in 1969, was building homes using timbers saved from old buildings for which a suburbanizing world no longer had purpose or room.

Nat Benjamin, after spending several years with his wife and young daughter delivering sailboats to the Caribbean and exploring the Mediterranean on their own boat, had settled in Vineyard Haven in 1972. Nat found work at the Martha's Vineyard Shipyard, all the while taking note of the small but increasing number of wooden sailboats that needed repair in the harbor.

The two men were casual friends, both in their late twenties and residents of Vineyard Haven. Both were builders and craftsmen, and most important, both thought there was nothing quite so useful, or delightful, than to work with a good piece of wood.

Now, on a spring evening in 1974, Ross and a few other friends came to the Benjamin home for a bon voyage dinner. The Benjamins' family boat, *Sorcerer*, a wooden, engineless ten-meter racing sloop built in 1921 in Norway, was tied up in Majorca, Spain. The sloop was being sold to an Island man who wanted her sailed to the Vineyard.

Ross made his first trans-Atlantic passage under sail, aboard *Sorcerer*, helping to successfully deliver the boat to Nat and his wife Pam, who used the proceeds from the sale of the boat to buy their Vineyard home.

Four years later, Ross came to Nat's house on a fall morning to ask for advice about *Urchin*, his wooden thirty-six-foot Casey cutter. With a friend, the late Ed Warsyk, Ross had hauled *Urchin* onto the beach at the head of the harbor using a cradle, rollers, planks, and Ed's Land Rover. The boat was bigger than the two Ross had owned and worked on earlier in his life, and important structural parts of *Urchin* were in pretty tough shape.

Nat and Ross chose the name of the boatyard quickly. Nat felt "Gannon and Benjamin" sounded rhythmically stronger than "Benjamin and Gannon," and both partners thought that calling the enterprise a "marine railway" would speak directly to owners of traditional vessels, who would most likely know that this was how old-fashioned yards hauled and launched boats.

◁ Nat, left, and Ross in the mid-1980s, unloading substantial planks of silver balli lumber for construction of a new boat. The builders pioneered the use of selectively harvested tropical hardwoods in the construction of wooden boats.

One of the first projects of the new boatyard is rebuilding *Venture*, a thirty-seven-foot gaff-rigged sloop built in 1910 and given to the Benjamins by a well-known Island sailor, Pat West of West Chop. Ross Gannon, right, works on *Venture*; the sloop required new frames, a new deck, a new stem at the bow and transom at the stern, among other substantial repairs. Below, the rebuilt *Venture* sails with family and friends.

# Nat

BY THE TIME he was twenty-two, Nat Benjamin had skippered a charter boat in the Caribbean for a season, delivered boats half a dozen times between New England and the West Indies, sailed across the Mediterranean single-handed and the Atlantic with a crew. He grew up with an older sister and brother in Garrison, New York, a small town on the Hudson River. As a teenager, Nat was restless – something was always calling him away on adventures.

He took a break from high school to work on a ranch in Texas and never went back. While working as an underage bartender in Newport, Rhode Island, he was invited to help deliver a thirty-two-foot sloop to St. Thomas. That trip, in the fall of 1967, set the course for the rest of Nat's sailing, designing, and boatbuilding life.

The following year, an owner in Long Island hired Nat to sail *Tappan Zee*, a wooden thirty-eight-foot schooner, from Malta to Newport. The odyssey took more than a year. Tempests blew out her

sails. Stress opened up seams in her hull. Her rigging let go. But as Nat sailed to Cueta, Spanish Morocco, and Casablanca for repairs, he discovered small, old-fashioned boatyards where sailors could work with skilled shipwrights and simple tools to get their boats going again.

"I liked the atmosphere, I liked the work," says Nat. "I could see the skills – lost skills, a lot of them. I knew that the chartering business was a good way to make pretty easy money. But I preferred this kind of work, and this kind of lifestyle, at those boatyards."

And once she was properly refit, *Tappan Zee* proved to be a splendid sea boat, like many of the other wooden boats Nat had sailed on open-water passages in his youthful career. Wooden boats were fun to work on and, if well thought out, saw you safely home like nothing else on the water. Why, Nat wondered, would anyone ever want anything less?

In the summer of 1972, he sailed into Vineyard Haven with his wife Pam, whom he'd met in the Caribbean, and daughter, Jessica, a toddler. The Benjamins were looking for charter work and a place to settle as a young family. They soon found a home near Vineyard Haven Harbor and in 1973 they had a second daughter, Signe, born at home. (Today Nat and Pam have five grandchildren.) At the house Nat set up a boat shop, and owners began to queue up with old sloops and catboats that needed repair. Nat began building dinghies and dories of his own, and he also started sketching larger traditional boats with an idea that here, in this harbor, he might one day soon get the chance to build them.

"For almost everything," he said in a 1977 interview, "there's usually a new and an old way to do things. And I've found it is cheaper, better and more fulfilling to do it with wood – the old way."

Most crucially, nearly all of *Urchin*'s frames – the structural ribs of the hull – needed to be replaced. This was a complicated process, requiring skill and swiftness. It meant heating six-to-eight-foot timbers of white oak in a steam box for just the right length of time, then – one after the other – pounding them quickly but forcefully down into the hull with a sledgehammer, and bending and clamping them to the shape of the frames they were to replace before they cooled too much and hardened. The frames were one and a half inch square, larger than any Ross had dealt with before, and he wanted counsel about how to work with them.

By then, Nat had earned a solid reputation for restoring wooden boats and building wooden dinghies and dories in a workshop at the family home, just up the road from the harbor. When Ross knocked on his door to ask for advice, Nat went one step further. He offered to help. "And he did," Ross recalls. "I just went to ask him a friendly question and get some advice, and he came down and helped me bend in almost every frame in the boat."

As Nat and Ross worked, they discussed all the other young men and women in town who needed help with old wooden boats of their own. Vineyard Haven, in the fall of 1978, was full of them.

In those days, Nat and Ross were young men living in an old and indispensable port of refuge on the southern New England coastline.

Until the opening of the Cape Cod Canal in 1914 – and depending on the direction from which the schooners, tugs, and barges sailed – Vineyard Haven was either the first or last harbor they could tuck themselves into on the perilous coastal highway between New York and Boston.

△ Nat and Pam, in the lower left corner, sail with President Clinton and First Lady Hillary Rodham Clinton aboard *Zorra*, a seventy-two-foot yawl rebuilt by the yard, in the summer of 1994. Chelsea Clinton steers with a bit of coaching from Nat.

Vineyard Haven is by far
the most commercially
and recreationally varied
harbor on Martha's Vineyard
and one of the most eclectic
on the eastern seaboard.
Along its shoreline – among
other businesses – lie three
boatyards, three marine
railways, a ferry terminal,
an oil storage facility, a
motel, a public beach, two
restaurants, a yacht club,
a newspaper office, a law
firm, an art gallery, a
supermarket, and scores
of waterfront homes.

▷ The topsail schooner
*Shenandoah* rests on her
mooring as a summer
sun rises over a glassy
Vineyard Haven Harbor.

For two hundred years, the traffic between these two towns had been heavy, and it picked up sharply during the Industrial Revolution: In 1883, for example, the *Cross Rip Lightship*, anchored ten miles east of Vineyard Haven as a sentinel in the very heart of Nantucket Sound, counted some twenty thousand passing vessels. Many ships dropped anchor in Vineyard Haven when the tides or weather went against them, or supplies ran low, or something broke on the voyage.

Vineyard Haven grew up on all this transient commerce. In the village of those days, there were lofts to mend sails; a shipbuilding company to repair hulls and rigging; a marine hospital; and a Seaman's Bethel to minister to sailors, body and soul – and sometimes spirit. Between 1865 and 1915, some two thousand ships were wrecked, and more than seven hundred lives lost, between Gay Head at the gateway to Vineyard Sound and Provincetown on the tip of the Cape. In Vineyard Haven there are two cemeteries where dozens of shipwreck victims, sometimes known but often not, were buried.

Vineyard Haven, called Holmes Hole until 1871, was also a town of shipbuilders. Beginning in the middle 1840s, the Holmes Hole Marine Railway – known today as the Martha's Vineyard Shipyard – built at least a dozen large schooners and brigs on a sandy isthmus dividing the harbor from an inland lagoon. Between the autumns of 1942 and 1943, thousands of feet of harbor shoreline were commandeered as an open-air construction site where shipwrights and house carpenters worked furiously to build barges and scores of high-speed rearmament and personnel boats for World War II. And for nearly forty years, between 1931 and 1969, a craftsman named Erford Burt, whose formal education ended after one week of high school, built many of the Vineyard Haven racing sloops that Nat Benjamin was restoring in his workshop in the late 1970s.

But what drew together the working past and wooden-boat building future of Vineyard Haven Harbor was the arrival of a topsail schooner named *Shenandoah* in July 1964. She was 108 feet on deck, carried 7,000 square feet of cotton canvas, and her two sharply raked masts towered over everything else on the water. Designed by her owner and master, Robert S. Douglas, who in a few years would build The Black Dog Tavern on the Vineyard Haven waterfront, *Shenandoah* was intended to take thirty passengers on weeklong cruises up and down the southern New England coastline.

A generation had passed since a commercial sailing vessel had called Vineyard Haven her homeport. *Shenandoah* was modeled on *Joe Lane*, a square-rigged revenue cutter that chased down pirates and tax cheats along the eastern seaboard in the middle of the nineteenth century. Like *Joe Lane*, *Shenandoah* had no engine. Kerosene lamps lit her saloon and navigation lights. Her stove was fired by coal, her dining room table was gimbaled to counteract the motion of the sea, and she carried a chanteyman who sang on deck when the schooner rode at anchor as the sun went down. Her passengers could experience nothing more authentic by way of old-world sailing ships in the twentieth century than a cruise on *Shenandoah*.

The Taylor/Simon family (and friends) aboard the newly completed *Sally May*, above. James and *Sally May* designer and builder Nat Benjamin share a moment of camaraderie at the water's edge.

PHOTOS BY PAM BENJAMIN

The first boat launched by the yard is the Canvasback sloop *Sally May*, also the first large boat Nat designs and builds. The boat is commissioned by singer James Taylor and named after his daughter, pictured with him. *Sally May*, intended to sail happily on Vineyard Sound, is also designed to explore the much shallower waters of Menemsha Pond.

# Ross

FROM THE AGE of three, Ross Gannon was taking things apart and putting them back together – radios, alarm clocks, whatever gizmos his parents gave him to work on. His father was an executive for merchandising at General Foods, and after moving around the country a bit, Ross settled with his parents and older brother and sister in Darien, Connecticut. When he was in seventh grade, he began to work summers at the Noroton Yacht Club. Under the direction of Charlie Potter, a math teacher who also supervised the maintenance of everything the club owned ashore and afloat, Ross began to find his way toward a career as an engineer and builder on land and water.

"What he did for us boys is, he let us do things that were so beyond our abilities," says Ross of his mentor. "He would just turn us loose. We built all the floats, we built all the ramps, we

replaced the deck on one of the launches one spring. We were teenage boys! Even if you botch it, you're having a ball. Doing it until it comes out right – I found that just fabulous. I gained a lot of confidence from working for Charlie Potter."

Ross earned a degree in engineering from North Carolina State University. He moved to the Vineyard, which he'd visited a few times, in 1969, after working for a company that trained dogs to look for land mines in Vietnam. On the Island, working his way up from smaller contracting jobs, he started moving and building houses, often using timbers salvaged from larger buildings he was being hired at the same time to demolish. He wanted to get back to the waterfront and repairing boats, though. "I thought in college or thereabouts how nice it would be to have a little boatyard," he says. "At the time I wasn't envisioning building boats. It would have been too far of a reach for me to imagine that. It was only at thirty or so that I thought, 'You know, I think I can do that.'"

He bought two old wooden boats, both day sailers native to the Vineyard, and began to teach himself how to repair them. His goal was to move up to a boat he could live on. He found her in *Urchin*, the Casey cutter he hauled on the beach in the summer of 1978 and went to Nat Benjamin to ask for advice about replacing her frames. Two years later, the Gannon and Benjamin Marine Railway was under way.

Ross has a son, Lyle, from a previous relationship, and twins Olin and Greta with his wife Kirsten Scott, to whom he proposed during the *Rebecca* project. At the boatyard, he long ago realized that he and Nat are ideally suited to building traditional boats together:

"My background is an engineering background, and I always approach things first with how to build it structurally, then how to do the rest of it – how to make it look pretty, how small you can make something and still have enough strength. And I think Nat starts with how he wants it to look and works the other way. So it's a wonderful combination. What we learn from one another, we take to the next job."

There were always among her crew each summer one or two traditionally minded young men who decided a harbor that supported a schooner like *Shenandoah* was a harbor they couldn't quite bear to leave. So they stayed, bought old wooden boats of their own – the only kind they would ever countenance, and the only kind most could then afford – and began to form an offshore neighborhood on Vineyard Haven Harbor. "In those days," says Gretchen Snyder, who would soon join Gannon and Benjamin as a sail maker, "there were about six of us living on boats, and you'd call over and say, 'What's for dinner?' It was a small community, and everyone did all their own work on their boats. It was very community-oriented, working together to get what we needed."

They were part of a larger collection of young nonconformists who were meeting in harbors up and down the Atlantic coastline and around the world. Many of these sailors of wooden boats heard about the harbor, some came to visit, and each year one or two stayed; by 1978 there were at least a dozen large wooden boats and many smaller ones in Vineyard Haven. But like Ross's cutter *Urchin*, a fair number were in poor condition, and their owners needed skilled plank-on-frame boatbuilders to help keep them on the water and under sail.

It took two days for Nat and Ross to reframe *Urchin* on the beach. By the end of the second afternoon, the men had decided to start a boatyard devoted to the repair and maintenance of wooden boats. "When we started our boatyard," says Nat, "it was really because of the clear evidence of this growing wooden boat

△ Ross works on *Liberty*, a forty-foot gaff sloop launched in 1986. For a few years, it was the largest boat built at the boatyard, and was designed by Nat Benjamin.

Three very different kinds of boatyard boats: The Benjamin family schooner, *Charlotte*, top, under construction; *Cassie*, a thirty-two-foot Cornish pilot rowing gig built with volunteers from the Vineyard Voyagers rowing group, above; and, right, the yard's first power boat, built for songwriter Jonathan Edwards and being launched into Vineyard waters.

*Lana and Harley*, top, now named *Calabash*, was at forty-four feet the first schooner the yard built. Bottom, *Rosalee*, commissioned by two-time Pulitzer Prize winner David McCullough, an Island resident.

LOUISA GOULD

Nat Benjamin designed the first boat for the fleet for Sail Martha's Vineyard, which since 1991 has focused on connecting the Island's schoolchildren and the community at large with the traditions and experiences of the Vineyard's maritime heritage. The eleven-foot Periwinkle was built in 1995 by Gannon and Benjamin; others were constructed using the plans, including two built in Island schools. All of the Periwinkles are still in use by Sail MV.

community in Vineyard Haven Harbor. Most of the wooden boats in Vineyard Haven are owned by tradesmen, schoolteachers – they're not people who can afford to say to the shipyard, 'Fix it.' Some are, but most of them aren't.

"So we wanted to help these people out, because we were part of them. We *were* them. And that was one of the main purposes of the boatyard – to provide a railway where, if people wanted to do their own work, fine; if they wanted some help, fine; if they wanted us to do everything, fine. But at least make it possible for people to work on their boats."

It took nearly two years to find the right waterfront lot and secure it with a lease. Just south of the beach where Nat and Ross had re-framed *Urchin* was a piece of land where some of the barges and rearmament boats were built during World War II. More recently, the town had fought off an attempt by a mainland entrepreneur to open a McDonald's there. In response to that threat, the town had restricted all new enterprises along the harborfront to marine use only.

During the summer of 1980 the partners began to organize a shop in a shed filled with old nets and cobwebs. They built a cradle and pier, acquired tools, rebuilt old machinery, laid down a railway to haul and launch boats, and cleared space upstairs for a sail-making loft.

As expected, traditional boats in Vineyard Haven began to line up right away for rebuilding and repair – a gaff-rigged sloop from 1904, a gaff-rigged Bahamian sloop from 1950 – but word of Gannon and Benjamin went out beyond the harbor breakwater, and soon Nat and Ross were working on a wooden commercial fishing boat from the neighboring Island harbor of Oak Bluffs and on a catboat that arrived in pieces from a boatyard in East Providence, Rhode Island.

It was also clear that Gannon and Benjamin was set up to do more than repair and restoration work. In 1980, there were few other boatyards in the country quite like it. Here was a self-sufficient operation, attending exclusively to boats of wood, hewing frames and planks from lumber and fastening them together with screws and nuts and bolts of bronze. Most distinctively, there was both a designer and an engineer in the shop who could build a new wooden boat to suit an owner's needs.

Given the Vineyard's long, proven, and nearly uninterrupted experience of traditional vessels, it should have been no surprise that the first boat launched by a yard set up to minister to old boats was, in fact, a new one. In August of 1980 Gannon and Benjamin christened *Sally May*, a twenty-five-foot Canvasback sloop, designed for singer James Taylor by Nat and built at Nat's shop the previous winter. As soon as *Sally May* was launched, there came an order for a twenty-foot gaff sloop, then a second Canvasback. As the two men began working together that first summer, Ross had figured that when the season ended, he'd go back to building houses until the following spring, when he and Nat both hoped more boats would come in for maintenance and repair.

"In the beginning," says Ross, "we never dreamed the boatyard would be full-time right from day one. But that first winter we had a new boat to build. Shocking!"

On a cold January afternoon, with the Mugwump shed still new and mostly empty of tools and gear, Nat bends a strip of wood, called a batten, on the loft floor, transferring his design from scale inches to full size, in feet, in the building where the schooner will be built.

lofting

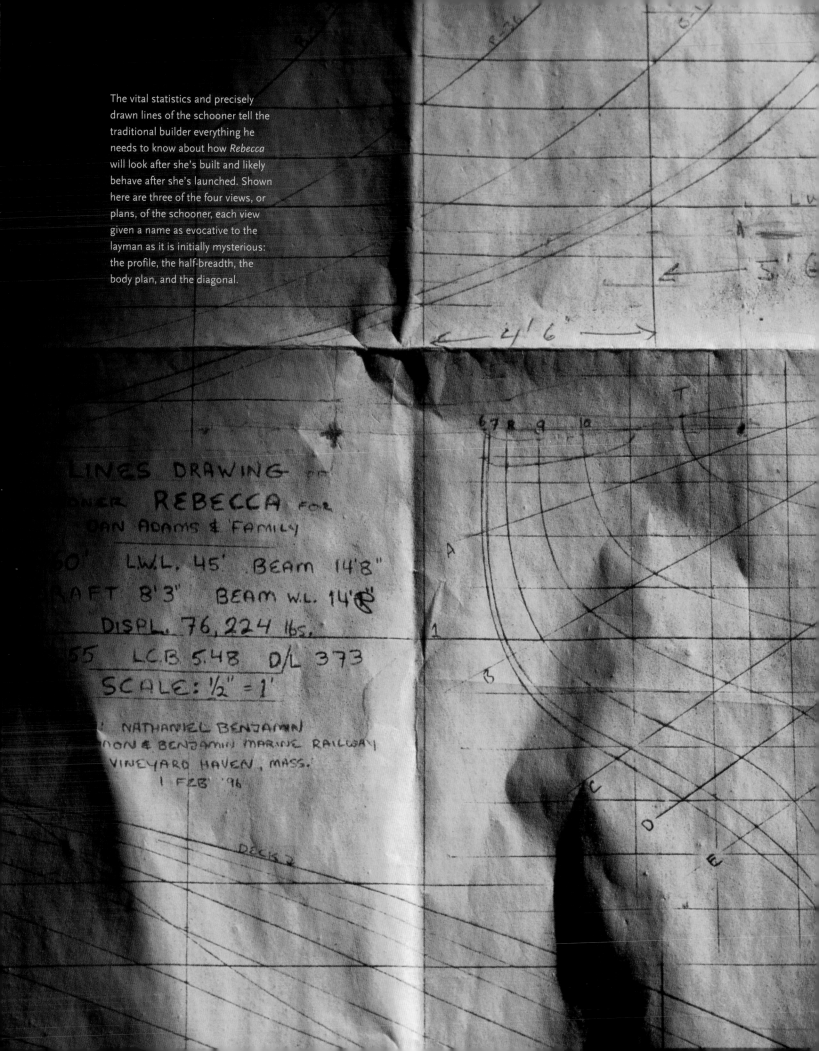

The vital statistics and precisely
drawn lines of the schooner tell the
traditional builder everything he
needs to know about how *Rebecca*
will look after she's built and likely
behave after she's launched. Shown
here are three of the four views, or
plans, of the schooner, each view
given a name as evocative to the
layman as it is initially mysterious:
the profile, the half-breadth, the
body plan, and the diagonal.

LINES DRAWING
REBECCA FOR
DAN ADAMS & FAMILY

60' L.W.L. 45' BEAM 14'8"
DRAFT 8'3" BEAM W.L. 14'8"
DISPL. 76,224 lbs.
55 L.C.B 5.48 D/L 373
SCALE: ½" = 1'

NATHANIEL BENJAMIN
NON & BENJAMIN MARINE RAILWAY
VINEYARD HAVEN, MASS.
1 FEB '96

DECK?

# *lofting*

For those who love traditional sailing vessels, there's nothing on the water quite so pretty or handy as the schooner rig. For Daniel Adams, who grew up always summering in Harwich on Cape Cod and who, now in his late thirties, is writing and directing independent films about underdog boxers and politicians fighting their unorthodox way to the top, a schooner is the boat he's dreamed of from boyhood.

It's the archetypal sailboat – two masts at least, the second (or mainmast) taller than the first (or foremast), and the sails usually rigged fore and aft, meaning from bow to stern. "There's nothing like a schooner for spreading canvas out," says Ross. "And then there's all of that history. Not just of schooner yachts, but of schooner fishing vessels and schooner trading vessels. Everybody harks back to that day and that era when you start talking about schooners."

In the fifteen years that have followed the establishment of the Gannon and Benjamin Marine Railway in 1980, the yard has built boats up to forty-four feet long, including its first schooner, for the international fashion designer Yohji Yamamoto. The yard has rebuilt or restored many more, including a schooner built for General George S. Patton and wrecked in a gale on the North Shore of Massachusetts; and a seventy-two-foot yawl, built in Italy and nearly destroyed by fire in Norfolk, Virginia. Wherever these boats sail, the reputation of the yard sails, too. All along the eastern seaboard, admirers come to think of boats designed, built, and restored by Gannon and Benjamin as inspiring, logical, enduring, and – as a natural result – great fun to sail.

Most important to both men, Nat and Ross have fully realized the dream they'd had in the summer of 1978. It's a yard where sailors can work on their own wooden boats, ask for help when it's needed, and turn over the most complicated projects to a team of craftsmen whose skills and point of view come from the same place as their own: out on the water and under sail. It is this reputation for advancing traditional boatbuilding values that brings Dan Adams to Gannon and Benjamin in the spring of 1995 with *Jane Dore III*, a handsome wooden ketch that Dan had bought pretty much on impulse in Florida and which he now thinks may need some work.

DAY I

Early January 1998: After more than two years of preparation, lofting begins at the Mugwump shed in Vineyard Haven.

SCHOONER: sailing vessel of two or more masts, the sails usually rigged fore-and-aft (along the centerline of the boat). "Schooner" may be a derivation of an old New England word: to "scoon" or move speedily.

# design

Today, most boat designers use computer programs to design. In his studio at the family home in Vineyard Haven, Nat draws by hand, relying on his experience, skill, and intuition to come up with plans that look handsome from every angle and serve all the purposes for which his boats will be used.

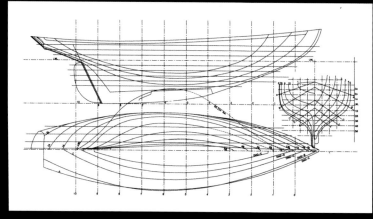

Nat uses the most elemental tools – a pencil, a protractor, colorful "ducks" to aid in drawing curved lines – to prepare the lines drawing of *Rebecca*, above, which shows multiple views of her hull and will be the guidelines for the plans that will be translated to wood.

Nat at his drawing table at his home office, where he will spend hours perfecting the plans for *Rebecca*. Nat has shelves of much-studied books on boat design close at hand for inspiration.

The loft floor, painted white but bathed in the glow of a wintry afternoon sunlight, serves as the canvas on which the lines of the schooner are drawn full size and faired, as well as the foundation on which *Rebecca* will be built. The lines in this photo serve as a giant graph paper on which Nat will soon plot his coordinates in order to transfer the plans as accurately as possible from drafting paper to loft floor.

A pair of nails holds a batten in place as lofting moves through the first month of *Rebecca*'s construction.

Permitting and construction of the Mugwump shed in Vineyard Haven occurs in record time for a large commercial property in the village, so eager are the town planning board and selectmen to see the Gannon and Benjamin boatyard expand its business on the waterfront. The yard applies for a building permit in July 1997, receives it a month later, and the shed is finished in November – five months from start to finish.

Dan hopes the boatyard can restore *Jane Dore* for a reasonable sum. Nat and Ross look her over and tell him that it will cost less to build the boat again from scratch than rebuild what's left; there is nothing to salvage but the doorknobs. Only if she is the boat of his dreams will it be worth the time, trouble, and money. For Dan, she is close to that boat, but not close enough.

The conversation turns to the schooner he's always imagined sailing: sixty feet on deck, able to sail powerfully at every angle to the wind, the sails divided up so that just two or three people can manage them all easily. A family boat with a saloon roomy enough for meals or games of backgammon, a small private stateroom for the owner, and a cozy forecastle – a living area on the boat pronounced foke-sul and often spelled *fo'c's'l* – at the bow where the current will gurgle by the waterline as children or guests bunk down to sleep. A boat that can cruise from the Caribbean to Maine and even cross the Atlantic without worry, heel comfortably in most any breeze, and move authoritatively through most every sea. And being a two-masted schooner built of wood, a boat that will arrest the attention of anyone who sees her beating into a harbor with every sail up.

Nat sketches the profile of the boat he thinks Dan envisions. In books and on the water, there are many historic American schooners to draw from, inspirationally and literally, and Nat Benjamin has studied them all. "That's the old-fashioned approach," says Antonio Salguero, Ross Gannon's nephew, a designer and boatbuilder in Port Townsend, Washington, who will be commissioned to build the schooner's masts. "And that's what Nat's doing. He's looking at other schooners and big boats of that size, length, width, and draft. He's asking, 'What is this boat going to be in relation to those?' That's how traditional designers do it."

There is, of course, the obvious question, one Nat and Ross answer every time a skeptic asks it, fearful that traditional boats cost more to build and maintain, leak all the time, and are archaic in an age when you can just pop a fiberglass hull out of a mold, all in one piece: Why build a boat out of wood?

"There's a New England Puritan ethic to Nat's designs," says Ginny Jones, then the Gannon and Benjamin office manager, "which means simple and traditional and nothing too fancy. Elegant simplicity. Virtually anyone who works in here has got an awful lot of ocean-going sea time under sail. It does lead to you knowing what works and what doesn't."

For Nat and Ross, this ethic starts with the hull. Early in their sailing and boat-building careers, each learned that wood is far easier to work with than fiberglass. If built traditionally, a wood hull lasts longer. If caulked skillfully, it's just about as watertight over time. If damaged accidentally, the repair is often more surgical and easy. And sailing a wooden boat feels more rewarding than fiberglass – an organic craft that seems to come to life as it moves through the water, rather than a plastic thing that seems vaguely to confront it.

The hull of a Gannon and Benjamin yacht is designed specifically for the wind and seas in which it will most often sail, with the trim on the hull handsome and spare. The deck is uncluttered and equipped with only the gear required. Everything on the spars and in the cockpit sits ready to hand and feels substantially built and reliably rigged. The sailor who asks Gannon and Benjamin to build him a boat values, above all, the interconnected virtues of simplicity, longevity, durability, safety, comfort, beauty, and happiness on any point of sail. The owners of most modern, fiberglass sailing yachts buy into something rather more elaborate.

▷ On a sheet of plywood, a batten outlines the shape of the propeller aperture (or space in which the propeller turns). The shape of the aperture has been traced onto a sheet of plywood beneath the batten, creating a pattern from which the actual structure of the aperture will be built.

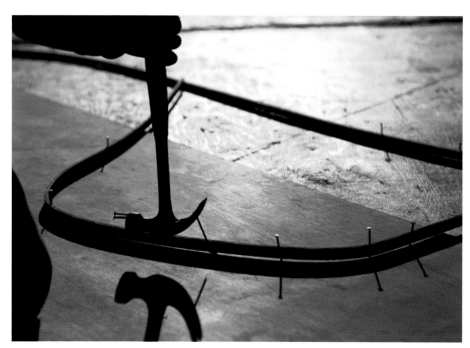

A batten and its shadow trace a curve in *Rebecca*'s hull. The loft floor shows the dark scars of nails driven earlier in the lofting process, as well as the scuffs from knees and boots as the builders toil on the plywood.

"The big fiberglass yachts – by that I mean over forty-five feet – they're built for a totally different market than ours," says Nat. *Rebecca* will be custom-built for a single client; fiberglass yachts come off a production line. And while a fiberglass boat of *Rebecca*'s size might start at roughly the same price as the schooner – about $800,000 – the costs will inevitably vector off in different directions from there.

"By the time it's all done," Nat says, "the glass boat will have air conditioning, heat, electronics up the yin-yang, a morass of wiring – which ensures not only that the boat will actually cost more than a million dollars, but that the annual maintenance will be staggering. Because all this stuff begins to disintegrate, and it'll be in and out of the builder's yard – which is all part of their planning – for the life of the boat, which might be ten or twenty years."

Nat and Ross have worked on wooden boats nearly one hundred years old and still sailing strong. Properly cared for, there is every reason to believe that this schooner, built at the turn of the twenty-first century, will still be sailing strong at the turn of the twenty-second. It is true that her amenities will be limited to the essentials, such as hot water, electricity, radar for the fog in Maine, a depth sounder, and a global positioning system. But the Gannon and Benjamin philosophy that simpler is better also means the schooner will spend much more time on the water under sail than in a boatyard under repair.

Dan approves the plans. The process of plank-on-frame construction begins – to the layman a craft as mysterious and complex as alchemy, to the traditional boatbuilder as simple, orderly, and accepted as anything in this world can be.

Boatbuilders are imaginative when it comes to meeting the needs of a lunch hour: On a winter's day, David Stimson heats up a pot of broth using a blowtorch. When Nat discovers he's left a spoon at home, he goes to a band saw and carves one from a piece of white oak.

*Rebecca* is too large to build at the boatyard on Vineyard Haven Harbor, so Nat and Ross lease a lot behind a shopping complex across the road and erect a shed for this project. Nat will mostly work here, Ross at the main yard. The shed is a long building with a peaked roof and rectangular windows set high under the eaves. Dan names the schooner *Rebecca* after his daughter and the shed Mugwump in honor of Republicans in the nineteenth century who abandoned corrupt candidates to vote for Democrats. In this new shed, Nat kneels on the loft floor – a plywood deck laid down over dirt and painted white, atop which *Rebecca* will be built.

Lofting is the vitally important first step in construction, and it takes days to do it right. The goal is to transfer the plans from Nat's drafting table to the shed, enlarging and "fairing" (roughly speaking, to unify and refine) them precisely from scale inches on paper to full length, width, and depth on the loft floor. There are, in fact, four plans or views of the schooner – the profile, the half-breadth (from below), the body plan (head-on of both bow and stern), and the diagonal (a set of lines that serve as a cross reference to those in the body plan). Each must be copied to the loft floor exactly, one atop the other in a huge web of overlapping views.

To establish his reference points, the first set of lines Nat copies across the floor is the grid from his plans, followed by the waterline of the schooner traced forty-five feet along the base of that grid. Then, working from his plans, reference points, and waterline, he copies and expands the four views onto the floor.

◁ Though hundreds of nails are driven into the floor during lofting, none remain there permanently. The lofting process soon yields to the time when patterns are made for important structural timbers in the hull, the first step in the construction of *Rebecca*. Here the load (or intended) waterline of the schooner is drawn in red for easy reference on a floor cluttered with other lines.

△ With lofting completed, construction moves on to making patterns for the frames of the schooner. Short lengths of wood are nailed to the loft floor along the shape of the faired lines of a frame. Plywood is slid into the gap between these wooden pieces and the floor, a batten is bent along their ends, and the line is traced onto the plywood, creating a pattern from which the frame will be built.

▷ The outline of *Rebecca*'s rudder may be seen in the two sets of nails as they curve on the loft floor. Working from the pattern for the sternpost, Nat measures the space in which *Rebecca*'s propeller will one day turn.

◁ With lofting completed and the patterns for the schooner's frames and other structured timbers cut, construction of the schooner may now begin.

"All these lines," says Nat, looking at them as they begin to lace over the plywood, "tell you things: how the boat's going to plank, how it's going to look, how it's going to go through the water." As he draws, Nat also fairs his lines, making sure each agrees in shape and dimension with the same line in the other views – and that all the lines look good. "You're moving lines a quarter of an inch here, an eighth of an inch there, maybe half an inch somewhere else," Nat says. "You're doing that through the whole lofting process."

To compare the lengths and shapes of corresponding lines in each of the four plans requires a ruler, but in boatbuilding nearly all the lines curve, so the ruler must be both quite long and almost infinitely flexible. From a worktable, Nat selects a batten – a slender length of spruce – and lays it on the floor near the bow. Along a line he likes the sweep of, he taps a series of nails. Against the nails he bends the batten, and with his pencil he ticks off those places where other lines drawn on the floor intersect it.

Now he moves the batten to the same line in the other views, making sure the intersecting lines in the first view cross the batten at precisely the same tick marks as in the others. Where they don't, he erases and redraws those lines until they agree in every way with the line he favors. As he erases and draws, the plywood dulls his pencil quickly. Over and over he carves the tip with a knife; accuracy demands that the lines on the loft floor be as fine as possible. At the end, the lines intertwine across the white canvas of the floor like the schematics for some vast invention by Leonardo Da Vinci.

Lofting *Rebecca* takes just six days – Nat tracing, moving, erasing, and redrawing the lines as methodically on the last day as he did the first. "That's one of the things that's fun about working with Nat," says David Stimson. He is a friend of Nat and Ross from Boothbay, Maine, who, in the vagabond spirit of many traditional boatbuilders, has brought his wife and two young sons to the Vineyard to help build a schooner whose size and provenance he may never have the chance to work on again. "Nat's done it so often before, and he knows his designs so well, that it was very easy to decide which of three lines he liked best, and make the other two do the same. Where he's the designer, he can do that. I think maybe that's why this was one of the easiest loftings I've ever experienced. It went quite smoothly."

The ancient Egyptians were building wooden ships at least by 2650 B.C. Centuries later, the Vikings perfected many of the characteristics of ship building seen in wooden boatbuilding today. Wooden boats have been used for travel, for defense by the armed forces, for fishing, for transporting cargo between countries, and for leisure, sport, and relaxation.

Compressed by the force of the bronze bolts that hold the heavy timbers together, a preservative and sealer called red lead seeps out between the seams where the forekeel fastens to the darker keel timber. The structure and weight of the schooner depends on the strength and integrity of the keel timber, the largest, widest, and longest in the boat.

3

keel

Nat and David Stimson lay
the keel timber. It is made of
angelique and is still wearing
the bright yellow dye marking
the Suriname mill from which
it shipped.

# *keel*

It's possible to think of the keel as the underwater wing of a sailboat. In concert with the wing aloft – the sail, drawing power from the breeze – as well as the shape of the hull at the waterline and below, the keel affects the balance, course, and even comfort of a boat as it works its way through wind and sea.

In *Rebecca*, the keel is an assembly of wood and lead running most of the way beneath the hull, and the backbone holding it all together is a single piece called the keel timber.

As the schooner heels over in the wind, the forces acting on this timber are substantial. The keel timber must support the structure of the hull as well as the thirteen-ton mass of the rest of the keel below – fully a third of the weight of the boat. Once cut to shape, *Rebecca*'s keel timber will measure nine inches from bottom to top, two feet across at its widest, and thirty-five feet from bow to stern.

In the Northeast, many traditional boatbuilders favor a keel timber hewn of white oak, which grows straight and tall and dense, holds a screw well, and resists rot. But these days, it's exceedingly difficult in the United States to find white oak of the breadth and length required to build a keel the size of *Rebecca*'s. So Gannon and Benjamin turns to the rainforests of Suriname, a small country on the northeast shoulder of South America, to find the essential lumber they need. Most important are the logs that will go into the keel timber, as well as those pieces that give shape to the bow (the forekeel) and stern (the horn timber).

In mid-January, while Nat and David Stimson loft the hull, a trailer arrives at Mugwump stacked with logs of angelique so massive the tires squash and squeal under the burden.

Lying on their sides, some of the logs measure wider and much longer than nearly anything seen on a construction site these days. The lumber is the color of an old penny, the grain straight and clear of checks, knots, and other faults. Where bark remains, it's pitted with age; where the bark is gone, the wood feels tough and smooth, like metal.

This is angelique, a tropical hardwood, finishing up a journey of twenty-six hundred miles by freighter, truck, and ferry from Suriname.

The angelique is stacked just outside the front door to the shed, and on a crisp day of scudding clouds, Nat and David identify and inspect it all closely, because

DAY 21

End of January 1998: Work begins to cut the keel timber. With this work done, *Rebecca*'s keel timber will measure nine inches from base to top, two feet across at its widest point amidships, and thirty-five feet from bow to stern.

Someone once asked the great literary wit Samuel Johnson what one book he would take with him if he were cast away on a distant island. His instant reply was, "Harrison's Elements of Boat Building."

△ *Rebecca*'s forekeel, which fastens to the keel and forms the structural shape of the lower part of the bow, is cut from another large angelique log. Angelique is exceptionally dense and rot-resistant, ideal for timbers that will bear such stress and remain below the surface of the water for much of the life of the schooner. The number "13" corresponds to the lumber list furnished by the sawmill in Suriname.

▷ Against the backdrop of the canvas that initially serves as the doorway to the Mugwump shed, the silhouette of the stem and forekeel timbers on the right, supported by a temporary brace and a rope from the rafters, outlines the shape of *Rebecca*'s bow. In the center, the curved shape of an assembled frame fills the canvas of the doorway to the shed. A band saw, a hammer, and a pair of paper containers holding screws and nails hint at the growing sense of industry and purpose at Mugwump as *Rebecca*'s form begins to take shape.

# ballast keel

THE BUILDINGS of the I. Broomfield and Sons manufacturing plant in Providence, Rhode Island, are built of cinderblock and painted the color of a chocolate bar. They stand on a service road between Interstate 95 and the harbor. Inside, there's the roar of furnaces, the shriek of steel sanders on lead, and in quieter places the flap of ventilator fans. The smell is fruity and sour, a mixture of stagnant water puddling on the concrete floor and of lead simmering in cauldrons around the building.

Broomfield has poured the lead keels for sailing vessels for more than fifty years. In a legacy from racing, the keel of a modern sailboat is often long and slender, like a fin, and finished at the bottom with a heavy bulb. The fin reduces drag, and the weight in the bulb allows the hull to be lighter and the rig to carry more sail. But a fin keel can act like a pivot point in a heavy sea, making the boat hard to steer. And setting so much weight so far below a light hull and extra sails adds to the stresses that can shorten the life of a boat.

△ At the I. Broomfield and Sons foundry in Providence, Rhode Island, workers re-heat the lead as it sluices from the furnace to the form of *Rebecca*'s 26,000-pound ballast keel.

*Rebecca*'s keel couldn't be more different. Running long and deep beneath the hull, her keel, built of heavy "deadwood" hewn of angelique and white oak, helps the schooner track purposefully and easily even in sharp and conflicting seas. But the keel has lead in it too – a long, massive plug bolted sturdily to the forward end of the wooden keel. Known as the ballast keel, it weighs 26,000 pounds, just over a third of the weight of the schooner as a whole. This is known as the ballast-to-displacement ratio, which helps to govern *Rebecca*'s "stiffness" – how much sail she can carry in a heavy wind, how quickly and far she heels over in the breeze, and how easily she drives through the chop. To Nat, a ballast-to-displacement ratio of 34 percent is just right for the feel of a family boat like this one.

Gannon and Benjamin sends Broomfield a wooden plug of the ballast keel. It's placed in a cask of liquefied sand about as wide as bathtub but three times longer. After the sand hardens, the plug is removed, leaving a mold into which the lead is poured. At 3:30 on a chilly morning in early April, the workers fire up the furnace, heating a cauldron to 700 degrees Fahrenheit, the pouring temperature of lead.

At eight o'clock, the lead begins to sludge down a chute to the mold. Two men dressed in protective suits stand on either side of it. As the lead fills the mold, the workers blast the surface with blowtorches to keep it from cooling unevenly. Under the flame, the lead turns black before going back to nickel gray. The job takes forty-five minutes, and though the lead will be hard by two o'clock, it will remain warm to the touch for several days. Ten days later, the ballast keel is removed from the mold. It's shipped to the Vineyard by truck and ferry, where it awaits an afternoon in early May when it will be backed under the keel timber and fastened to the hull it will stabilize for the rest of *Rebecca*'s days.

for the life of this schooner the wood from a few of these logs will serve as the foundational timbers in the hull.

Nat and Ross pioneered the use of tropical hardwoods in traditional hulls in 1982, when the boatyard was only in its third year. Brad Ives, a friend of Ross's, was freighting goods, including wood for houses, around the world in a one-hundred-foot sailing vessel named *Edna*. Brad had just begun to buy tropical hardwood from loggers and millers in Suriname, and he was sure they could find, select, harvest, and mill exactly the sort of stout, rot-resistant, sometimes idiosyncratically shaped timber that plank-on-frame construction demands.

△ *Rebecca*'s forekeel and timber keel, awaiting delivery of her ballast keel from Rhode Island, rest in the Mugwump shed as spring approaches. Floor timbers of angelique, to which the base of the schooner's frames will soon be fastened, parade like vertebrae down the backbone of *Rebecca*'s hull.

Bracing himself on a floor timber to the right and a stern timber to the left, Nat, using an auger bit, prepares to drill a keel bolt through the stern timbers. Hanging from the rafters behind Nat is the framework of a twenty-eight-foot war canoe being built by David Stimson in his spare time for the Pine Island Camp of Belgrade Lakes, Maine.

"What I like about it," says Nat, surveying the angelique, "is that the mill owners and sawyers down there have to go into the forest to look for the specific wood we need. Some trees have to be crooked for certain pieces in the boat, a lot of them have to be certain lengths, some have to be a certain type of growth. That, to me, makes the wood more valuable, because they can't just clear-cut it."

In front of the shed, Nat and David chainsaw the keel timber, the machines screaming in the cold air as they bite into the dense angelique. With the log hewn roughly to shape, they each use an adze – a tool with a wide, curved bit – to smooth the roughest places left behind by the chain saws, and then planes to smooth them even more. The job of cutting and trimming the log takes three days. When that work is done, the keel timber is ready to move into the Mugwump building.

At the main yard, Ross and his crew have begun work on the first boat in a new class of small sloops designed by Nat. But they come over to Mugwump to help push the keel timber on rollers into the center of the shed, raise it with jacks, remove the rollers, and lower it onto blocks of wood on the plywood floor. With this, the momentum of the *Rebecca* project shifts meaningfully inside the building: Moments before, the schooner existed only in theory, as a latticework of faired lines on the loft floor. Now the largest single timber in the hull anchors the space where the rest of the schooner will be built.

At the time *Rebecca*'s keel is laid, there is no other boat of her size and rig being built of wood, plank-on-frame, anywhere in the United States.

◁ A portrait of force in motion: A large keel bolt is hand-driven into a stern timber.

△ Scoured by a sander, the ballast keel fits tightly against the deadwood of the wooden keel. The ballast keel, at 26,000 pounds, accounts for more than a third of the weight of the vessel as a whole.

The keel of *Rebecca* has been laid, a milestone in the life of any boat.

Nat looks around the Mugwump shed. The work tables have begun to fill with tool boxes; heavy lengths of line; boxes of nails, bronze screws, nuts, and bolts; handsaws; hammers; metal files; chalk lines; notepads and pencils; battens and scrap wood left over from construction of the shed just a few months earlier. On the plywood floor he sees the lines of the lofting, already beginning to fade along with the white paint, under the footfalls of the boatbuilders' boots. And in the middle of the shed he sees the keel timber of this, the first vessel to be built under its roof. The sky is blue, the wind still, and for the first time in a week it's milder outside the shed than in it. He and David take their brown-bag lunches and head for the door and sunlight.

"Yeah," he says with a smile, "now it's looking more like a boat shop."

# rudder

Building *Rebecca*'s rudder, which begins with the cutting of patterns during lofting, carries on through most of the construction. The rudder is massive — about eight feet long, three inches wide at the leading edge, and three-quarters of an inch at the trailing edge.

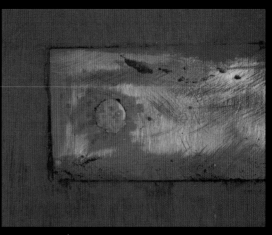

◁ Like the keel timbers, the rudder is built of angelique. At left, Nat drives a bronze drift, or heavy pin, through the trailing edge. Above, one of the rudder straps, which holds the structure to the stern timbers.

◁ The large fitting shaped something like a bow tie is called a butterfly, which ties together the sternpost and the keel timber. The fittings are fabricated from patterns made at the shop and cast in bronze at a foundry on the mainland.

The size, shape, and strength of *Rebecca*'s hull become clear after her most substantial frames are set up. Running across the hull, temporary planks (which boatbuilders call cross spawls) reinforce the tops of the frames until the deck beams are built and fastened into place.

framing

A sawn piece (or futtock) of white oak, which will make up the upper half of a double-sawn frame. For reasons of strength, boatbuilders, who deal so often with curved timbers such as this one, want the grain to follow the curve whenever possible.

I t's late March now, unusually brisk for the Island. Nat and David Stimson, still working alone, lay the pattern for a frame on a low wooden table right outside the door. The keel timber lies a few feet away, in the center of the shed. Bolted partway down the length of the keel runs a parade of floor timbers, inverted trapezoidal blocks of dark angelique that serve as vertebrae to the rigid backbone of the hull.

The builders will fasten the base of *Rebecca*'s framing to these floor timbers in the same general way a ribcage joins a spine.

Against a wall, a stack of frames stands head high. Some are long and curved, like an elongated scythe; others, higher in the stack, are shorter, the curve a little less pronounced. These frames are all double-sawn, so called because they're made up of two timbers fastened together, face to face, for durability. Short or long, double-sawn frames are all about strength.

For nearly twenty years, Nat and Ross have framed new boats exclusively with steam-bent ribs – the long, slender type that they will heat and bend into much of *Rebecca*'s hull. But where the curves and stresses are most severe, *Rebecca* is large enough to also warrant double-sawn frames, much heavier and less flexible than steam-bent. This schooner represents a milestone for Gannon and Benjamin – the first boat built by the yard using frames of two different types.

"Cutting double-sawn frames is something we learned rebuilding *When and If*," says Nat of a schooner whose reconstruction at the yard five years before added a few pages of history to a vessel that was historic from the start.

*When and If* is a sixty-four-foot Alden-designed schooner built in 1939 for General George S. Patton and his wife Beatrice to sail around the world "when and if" he returned from the next world war. During a November gale in 1990, she was thrown onto the rocks at Manchester-by-the Sea, Massachusetts, leaving a hole in her port side you could push a Cadillac through sideways. The insurance company wanted to chainsaw the boat, but Nat and Ross admired her design, construction, and past, and thought she could be rebuilt. With a partner, they bought and barged her down to the boatyard.

*When and If* was built entirely of double-sawn frames, and the rocks had shattered seventeen of them on her port side. At first Nat and Ross puzzled over

**DAY 50**
Early February 1998: Pattern-making for the first of *Rebecca*'s double-sawn frames begins. Pattern-making continues through March, and the actual building of these heavy-duty frames starts immediately afterward.

At the start of framing, Nat expects that at this pace, it will take a year and half to build *Rebecca* – fast for a small crew, but slow compared to the old days: "Keep in mind that up and down the coast of this country, especially in New England, clipper ships were built in an average of ninety days. This boat could sit on a clipper ship's deck. We have no concept of the kind of work that used to be cranked out."

JOHN BLANDING, THE BOSTON GLOBE

▷ *When and If*, a schooner built for General George S. Patton in 1939, is wrecked in a gale at Manchester-by-the-Sea, Massachusetts, in November 1990. After the accident, Nat and Ross, seen opposite lashing her forestaysail after the restoration, purchased the schooner in partnership with another owner and rebuilt the boat in Vineyard Haven. Above, they re-launch the boat.

how to duplicate them. Then they hit upon a simple, ingenious solution – copy the structure and form of the corresponding, undamaged sawn frames on her starboard side and fasten them the opposite way on her port. The nearly miraculous ease with which these frames were patterned, built, and replaced convinced both men of their virtue in the construction of larger boats.

"Double-sawn, one advantage is, they're very strong," says Nat. "They're relatively easy to make because you don't need any real long pieces of wood, and you can make the frames up right on the loft floor. Get the frames set up on the keel, and it eliminates having to make molds out of pine boards, or something else, to get the curves in the hull. The disadvantages are, a sawn frame is much bigger and heavier and more expensive. It's not as neat. It's not as clean.

"Steam-bent frames are very nice, because they're full length, so the grain follows the shape of the hull. Steam-bent frames are cheaper to put in. They're a little bit lighter. You don't need such a big frame to get the same amount of strength because it's one continuous piece of wood. But the stock has to be absolutely flawless; it can't have the tiniest little knot in it, because you have to bend it and it might not bend. It might break."

*Rebecca* will have twenty-three sets of double-sawn frames, set up every four and a half feet along her waterline and on either side of her masts. But Nat and David need help standing up the frames, bolting them to the floor timbers, and fairing them – "fairing" in this case meaning to adjust the ribs so they line up as designed from bow to stern and side to side. Of course, Nat and David also need help to build the rest of the boat.

It's time to hire a crew.

△ A double-sawn frame under construction: The upper and lower pieces (or futtocks) of the frame are clamped so that they may be permanently fastened together and set up on *Rebecca*'s keel.

◁ A vertical approximation of the shape of *Rebecca*'s hull reveals itself in the various shapes of the double-sawn frames, completed and stacked along a wall at Mugwump.

Gannon and Benjamin is known around the boatbuilding world; young men and the occasional young woman make pilgrimages across the country and from as far away as Britain, France, Finland, Australia, and New Zealand, to learn traditional techniques at the yard. "There's nothing very complicated here," says Nat. "It's all basic carpentry, but if somebody comes in who wants to be a boatbuilder who's never shingled a roof, or put in a window, or fixed a toilet, they're going to be at a big disadvantage."

Among the first hired to work on *Rebecca* is Todd McGee, a veteran boatbuilder at twenty-six who has recently helped rebuild *Alabama*, a ninety-foot pilot schooner built in 1926. *Alabama* belongs to Bob Douglas and, with his *Shenandoah*, sails out of Vineyard Haven with passengers on day cruises. There's also Casson Kennedy, twenty-three, who has no boatbuilding experience but has worked as a Vineyard stonemason.

Now numbering four, the crew hoists frames onto the keel and through-bolts them to the floor timbers. Casson marvels at his early lessons in plank-on-frame construction.

"They have to be plumb, square to the centerline, and they must measure correctly off each other," he says. "You have these three dimensions of 'twistability' – and also the possibility of three dimensions of error. When you're putting them together, there isn't really a fixed point in space yet, so it's interesting to see where you build 'out' from. It seems to be the centerline, drawn fore and aft on the keel. That's how we got the perpendicularity." He smiles. "But I'm not sure yet." Casson tries to keep his questions to a minimum and learn just by doing, as Nat and David suggest.

The crew bolts the last double-sawn frame to the keel in the middle of May. With the structural pieces called the forekeel and horn timber now slanting upward at either end of the backbone, establishing the rake of the bow and counter at the stern, these ribs, looked at head-on, begin to outline the wineglass shape of the hull. Their skeletal sturdiness suggests not only how long the builders intend *Rebecca* to sail – generations – but also what she'll be ready to face by way of wind and water as she does: pretty much anything.

It's the third week in July, a hot day, the sky creamy. A teenager who's spent the first half of the summer working at the main yard comes to Mugwump to apologize to Nat. The boy says he can't stay to help with the *Rebecca* project as promised today; he's been invited to go sailing on *Alabama*. "What!" Nat cries with a laugh. "You're going out on *Alabama* when you could be here steam-bending frames?"

It's hardly a fair choice: What's about to happen now amounts to a race, one of the few moments in the schooner project when things must happen quickly as well as properly, or they just won't work.

The steam box is fastened to an outside wall of the shed. Built of wood, it's a simple device – about eighteen inches wide by fifteen feet long. A small tank of propane heats a kettle, and steam rises through a black rubber tube into the box.

Wearing workman's gloves, Nat opens the door, reaches in, and backs away with a heated twelve-foot length of white oak. At two and a half inches square, the

△ Double-sawn frames are made up of futtocks – curved pieces of various lengths – that are fastened together with wooden pins, top, called tree nails (or trunnels for short). These are cut from locust, measure about three-quarters of an inch in diameter, and are slightly tapered. After drilling a hole and driving in the trunnel, the exposed end is split and a wedge of purpleheart, bottom, is forced into it to hold the trunnel securely in place.

A plumb bob, hung from a reinforcing timber called a cross spawl, helps the crew determine whether the sawn frames are properly balanced in all dimensions.

△ Nat works with a heated frame prior to bending it into the hull. *Rebecca*'s steam-bent frames are fashioned from timbers of clear white oak measuring two and a half inches square. Where the turns in the hull are most severe, the steam-bent frames are "kerfed," or cut along their lengths, to relieve some of the tension on the grain.

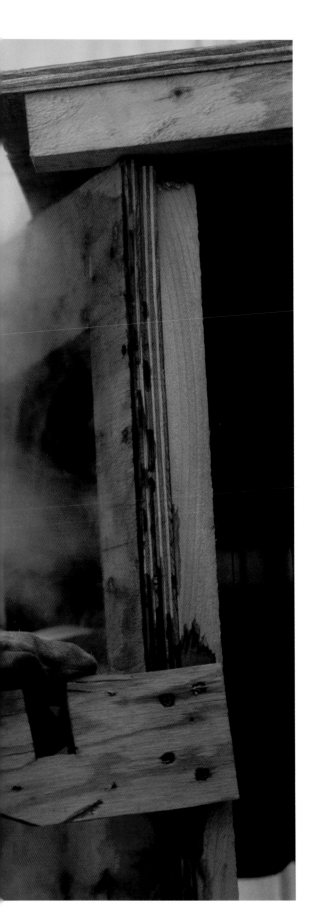

◁ Nat and Mark Laplume retrieve a frame from the steam box, fastened along an outdoor wall of the Mugwump shed. In a technique known as composite construction, often favored in traditional boatbuilding by the British, and in a few other European countries, *Rebecca*'s framing is a mixture of heavy sawn and lighter steam-bent ribs.

▷ The crew installs a steam-bent frame at *Rebecca*'s bow. Running the length of the hull are temporary supports called ribbands, which help hold the sawn frames in place before planking and to which the malleable steam-bent frames are clamped until they cool and harden in place.

"Book learnin' takes a while, but hand learnin' takes a lifetime."

—DAVID STEVENS, *a Nova Scotia farmer with a ninth-grade education who at thirty-eight took up boatbuilding and built more than seventy boats, among them some of the swiftest schooners on the Atlantic coast.*

timber looks no bigger than the leg to a heavy dining room table. Along with a clutch of other frames, it's been cooking in the box for an hour per inch, Nat's recipe for steam-bent frames. When he rests the middle of the frame on his shoulder, the ends sag with rubbery lassitude, and the grain actually shivers along its length with each step he takes into the shed.

Staging surrounds the schooner, a girdle of wood announcing, more immediately than anything else up to now, that *Rebecca* is a construction site. Casson Kennedy and Brad Ives stand on the scaffolding, and Casson holds a sledgehammer. Inside the hull, caged within the sawn frames, is Todd McGee, crouching on the floor timbers. With him are two new members of the crew, Ted Okie and Mark Laplume. Everyone wears gloves. Nat hands one end of the ribbonlike frame up to Casson and Brad, who lift the end into the rafters, where it sways drunkenly and steams with heat and moisture.

The builders have perhaps five minutes to force this slender frame into place, pounding, bending, clamping, and twisting it along a narrow, tortuous pathway from the deck all the way down to the keel timber. Wait too long and the frame will cool and split rather than yield to the wanted shape. The pathway is defined on the outside of the hull by lengths of spruce called ribbands, which temporarily run along the face of the sawn frames and will be removed one at a time as the hull is planked.

On the inside of the sawn frames, the pathway is bordered by two heavy, permanent, reinforcing timbers of angelique – the sheer clamp up near the deck, the bilge stringer down near the waterline.

Casson and Brad insert the end of the first frame, and it slides easily past the sheer clamp and the uppermost ribband, then past two angelique planks fitted early to the hull, then the next eight ribbands, until it reaches Nat on the loft floor. He pulls the frame outward against the ribbands, and Todd, Ted, and Mark swiftly clamp it to the every second or third one, firmly enough to hold the shape but gently enough so Casson and Brad above can keep pushing it downward. The grain yields elastically.

The frame begins to reverse its curve below the bilge stringer, the reinforcing timber at the waterline. Todd, Ted, and Mark pull on the heel of the frame from inside the hull, Nat pushes from the outside, and Casson and Brad shove downward from on high. Every face turns red with effort.

Suddenly there's a crunch, like the sound you hear in your head when you bite down on dry cereal. The reverse curve is too much for the frame, though it is still hot. The wood splits up the grain from the base. The men have lost about two feet from the bottom. But they've cut it extra long just for this reason. Todd quickly saws off the split in the timber, and Casson whangs on the top of the frame with his sledgehammer, forcing it downward inch-by-inch onto the floor timber, where Todd clamps it into place.

One steam-bent frame down. Fifty-nine to go.

◁ Ted Okie works on a floor timber in *Rebecca*'s bow. The skeleton of the hull is now fully outlined by a combination of frames – double-sawn in the foreground, single-sawn adjacent to Ted, with three sets of lighter steam-bent frames between them. Across the floor timbers lies the foremast step, the foundation of the mast.

An old (or maybe not so old) saying: If God wanted aluminum boats and fiberglass boats, he'd be growing fiberglass trees and aluminum trees. And he doesn't.

Now planked and caulked,
*Rebecca*'s hull takes on
substance as well as form.
The waterline of the schooner
is visible where the white hull
paint meets the orange primer
coat on her bottom.

planking

Casson Kennedy lifts a garboard (the lowest) plank to the hull. The garboard is a particular concern to traditional boatbuilders because of the stresses and curves in this area of the hull. *Rebecca*'s is hewn from a single length of angelique.

# planking

In August the reeds just beyond the open door to the Mugwump shed sway and hiss in a warm breeze off the lagoon. Inside the building, the shape of the hull that the skeletal framing only hinted at a month before begins to reveal itself, plank by plank, as the crew sheathes it from keel to deck.

"I love putting on the first two or three planks," says Ross, who comes to Mugwump with business for Nat. "There's nothing more rewarding than watching the shapes develop as you're twisting and bending them on there."

For Ross, it has been a busy summer at the main yard, too. He and the crew have just launched the second in a class of twenty-one-foot sloops for one Vineyard client and are now working on an eleven-foot tender for another. He looks up at the sweep of *Rebecca*'s hull. Todd McGee and Casson Kennedy lift a plank, and Ted Okie and Mark Laplume clamp the ends to the sawn frames. "But by the time you've put the twentieth plank on," he adds, "you can't wait to see the end of it. It's the same with every part of boatbuilding because so much of it is repetitive."

Nat slowly pushes a plank into the mouth of a planer. David stands on the other side, ready to catch it. The goal, through many runs, is to shave each plank down to one-and-seven-eighths inch. As the timber trembles its way through the machine, the wail is tremendous. To either side, the shavings — mauve from the angelique planks fastened high along the sheer line and low along the keel, and off-white from the silver balli planks in between — have been gathered into two gerbil-nest piles, both waist high.

Silver balli, another wood selectively harvested in Suriname, is rich in oil like teak but much less expensive. Oil reduces the amount of water that can seep into the grain, lowering the risk of rot. The builders want each plank to be as long as possible to minimize the number of joints (called butts), which can move and leak. But because planks twist as they run along the hull, there can be no defects — no sapwood, no worms, nothing that can fracture or decay over time. To make sure the schooner project has enough planking, Nat has ordered twice as much silver balli as the builders would need if all of it had been perfect. What's left over will be trimmed to rid it of problems and used in the bulkheads.

DAY 205

August 1998: First garboard (or lowermost) plank is fastened to the hull. Caulking (or sealing) of the hull begins after the planking is finished, some seventy days later.

Just inside the door of the Mugwump shed stands a planer, heavily framed in iron, its motor quietly humming. The manufacturer's plate reads "S.A. Woods Machine Company Boston Mass. U.S.A. Patented . . . June 3, 1890." It's one example, among many, that Gannon and Benjamin believes machines and tools were built a bit better in the old days. In traditional boatbuilding, it's the oldest things that often work best.

△ During the first summer of construction, Nat measures an angelique plank on the lot in front of the Mugwump shed. When planed and faired, *Rebecca*'s planking will finish at one and three quarters inch thick.

▷ Casson Kennedy clamps a silver balli plank to a double-sawn frame prior to fastening. To add strength to the structure of the hull, the builders stagger where the ends (or butts) of the planking meet.

Mark Laplume planes the bottom of a silver balli plank as the planking further reveals the sweep of the schooner's lines at the bow. The zig-zag pattern represents the places where the planks have been screwed into the framing.

◁ Todd McGee, left, and David Stimson clamp the sheer (or uppermost) plank to *Rebecca*'s hull. Because of the weight of the keel below and the tension of the rigging above, the lowermost and uppermost planks bear more stress than the planks between them. The builders choose dense angelique for these important strakes in the planking.

The humor of boatbuilders: When a visitor asks David Stimson whether he considers traditional boatbuilding at all hazardous to the health, David says no, then surreptitiously palms a fistful of wood shavings, puts them to his nose and mouth, and sneezes them six feet across the shed.

Each plank curves in a unique way as it runs along the framing, and the outboard face of each sawn frame has been individually and precisely beveled so the planks lie fair – smoothly, without humps or flat sections – against them. The top of each plank is also beveled to fit snugly against the right-angled bottom of the plank above. And each joint is reinforced on the inside with a butt block where the planks meet end to end. No plank is more complex than the garboard, a weighty single timber of angelique that lies just above the keel. The garboard widens markedly at the stern to cover the added girth in the low, aftermost sections of the boat.

The outside of the planks is still rough when fastened to the frames; the inside faces of the planks have been backed out (or cut) to match the curve of the frames.

With the job complete at the end of September, the builders begin to plane and sand the outside face of the frames by hand, the silver balli lightening with each run over the grain. Especially hard to reach is the area amidships, below the waterline. Todd, Casson, Ted, and Mark duct tape thick pads of packing foam around their knees and kneel on staging planks. Their spines twist left and right, and their necks arc backward under the gentle, spreading belly of the schooner, as they plane and sand the planks over their heads.

At the end of the day, Todd's head and shoulders are shrouded in shavings. He wears a mask to keep the dust out of his throat and lungs. His face is mummified with silver balli powder and sweat. He steps from under the hull, rolls his shoulders, bends at the waist, stretches his back, and looks around for a different plane. It's inside the hull, so he must climb the staging and go over the rail to find it.

"It's harder to get in and out now," he says, looking along the length of the hull. *Rebecca* is all planked up.

Like the main yard across the street, Mugwump has begun to attract visitors who have heard about a historic schooner being built on Martha's Vineyard and want to see how it's done. Parents bring young children, who stand shyly at the

From the staging around the hull, Frank Rapoza, a master caulker who learned his trade as boy in South Dartmouth, Massachusetts, uses a caulking mallet and iron to set cotton into the seams between the planking at *Rebecca*'s bow. Red lead, a preservative, fills those seams that have already been caulked.

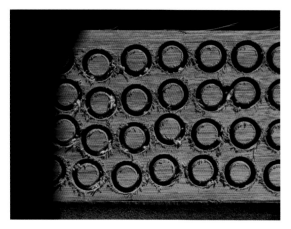

△ Forrest Williams, top, paints *Rebecca*'s hull. Bungs, above, cut from a plank, will be used to cover the holes produced by the screw that fasten the planking to the frames.

△ A fire on the night of Tuesday, October 17, 1989 – years before the Mugwump shed was built or *Rebecca* was commissioned – destroyed the boatyard. Fund-raisers, donations of machinery and tools, and a community-led shed-raising put Gannon and Benjamin back in business three months later.

shed door until invited in for a closer look. Nat or David stop work to discuss the dimensions of the hull, the weight of the lead in the keel, the places the schooner will go, the sort of wood they're using – and why they're using wood to begin with.

"They've earned a lot of good will," says Whit Hanschka, a blacksmith in Tisbury, of Gannon and Benjamin, where he worked through most of the 1990s. "You see it in the range of their customers. Everyone from the seriously rich people who have them build new boats, to the fishermen, to the random house-carpenter types who need something funky. Nat and Ross will always drop everything and spend a half-hour talking about whether to use teak or mahogany on some project, where the guy doesn't know the difference between spruce and fir. Who knows, maybe that's why they're not rich men at this point. But people like them. If you do that for ten or fifteen years, then people begin to realize that you're genuine."

To the extent that anyone has ever considered this help a favor, it was repaid in full after the night of Tuesday, October 17, 1989, when, for reasons unknown, the main yard burned. Fed by lumber, shavings, linseed oil, and the hulls of several boats, the inferno left the building looking like a meteorite had hit it.

Vineyarders appeared with offers of help at dawn the next day. They gave the builders tools their grandfathers had used. They placed orders for boats and sails, paying in advance. They lent office space, donated sewing machines, held benefit dinners and a concert that included James Taylor and his talented siblings. On the morning of Saturday, November 11, a shed-raising was scheduled. Nat thought two dozen people might show up. He arrived at eight o'clock to find at least thirty

Depicted in a photo tacked up in later years on the shed wall, *Corineus*, a twenty-eight-foot pilot cutter, center, is launched during the blaze and saved. *Java*, a fifty-seven-foot yawl, left, is a total loss, as are all the smaller boats under the shed and in the shop.

▷ Viewed from below, the forekeel of *Rebecca*'s newly planked hull is framed by two levels of staging and by the deck planking lying on the racks to either side of the schooner. Once most of the interior is built, these lighter planks will cover the deck in much the same way the planking has covered the hull.

"A wooden ship has the anatomy of a living body. There is a backbone. . . ribs. . . muscles and tendons (the rigging) and skin (the planking), and a vast number of pieces and sections named after parts of the body."
— PETER H. SPECTRE
*Wooden Ship*

Fastened, bunged, and caulked, a set of angelique planks sheathe *Rebecca*'s hull. With the hull planked, attention soon turns to building the interior of the schooner.

master carpenters and hundreds of regular folk ready to build. That morning the framing lay on the ground. Two days later they were shingling the roof.

"I remember Ross was quoted in the paper as saying he never realized they were a successful boatyard until they burned down," says his nephew, Antonio Salguero. "I think that fire instilled in them a stronger sense of their place in the community, instead of being just some business on the waterfront, make or break, season by season. They were always stronger than that – they had a following at that point. But I think it clarified in their own minds that they had a clientele that was as strong as friends."

"I think cotton is very much underappreciated in a wooden boat like this," says David as caulking begins in October. At the moment, light slits through the seams up and down the hull and all along it; now comes the time to seal it up tight.

It's clear David enjoys this part of boatbuilding, working with mallet, cotton, and flat steel tools of varying widths called caulking irons. "People don't understand what the function of cotton is. It's not just to keep water out. A hull like this with no cotton in it would be just limber as can be. Get all that cotton in there and you've put tons of pressure between each seam. It turns the thing into one rigid structure. It acts like a truss. You can actually hear the difference while you're caulking the vessel. When you're starting off, it's kind of a hollow sound, and by the time you're all done, the boat is almost ringing like a bell because it's so tight."

Frank Rapoza, who learned caulking during his boyhood at the Concordia Boatyard in South Dartmouth, Massachusetts, leads the crew. As they have for weeks now, the men begin the day by taking sandpaper to the planks. They sand away fuzzy places on the edges where the cotton might catch. They use reefing hooks to dig out grit between the seams.

For all the seams but the lowest five, the boatbuilders insert two strands of cotton into the seams. Using two types of caulking irons, these strands are looped into loose coils and driven (the caulker's word is "tucked") into the seams. The number of tucks varies according to the width of the seam – the wider the seam, the more closely spaced the tucks. David guesses that by the time the crew is done, *Rebecca* will have two hundred pounds of cotton set into the seams of her hull.

The bottom five seams are first filled with a strand of cotton and one or two strands of oakum, which is made up of tarred, coarse hemp fibers. Oakum resists the degrading effects of diesel fuel, which can seep into the seams if it spills into the bilge from the fuel tanks. The caulked seams are then painted with a coat or two of red lead (a primer and preservative), and then puttied to seal the job up tight. Above the waterline, the hull is given its first coat of white paint – like red lead, a primer to keep the wood from drying out while the rest of the hull is built.

These first coats of color foreshadow the livery that the schooner will wear on her launching day – a brilliant white hull set off sharply by a bottom of royal red. Meantime, another milestone comes on the October evening when a mallet and caulking iron strike a last ringing blow against the schooner's hull:

Now *Rebecca* can float.

The last plank to be fastened to a wooden boat is called the shutter plank, and the festivities to celebrate this milestone, the shutter party. Two dozen people attend *Rebecca*'s shutter party on the evening of Tuesday, September 22, 1998.

The evolving interior of *Rebecca*, as seen through the deck beams and entranceway to the forward deckhouse: Within the hull, bulkheads begin to define living spaces, and lockers and cabinets take shape on either side of the hull. On deck, silver balli planking begins to cover the deck beams, and light from within the hull illuminates the hole for the mainmast.

interior

Nat tests the fit of a cabin top beam, fashioned from black locust and dovetailed into the sides of the forward deckhouse. The larger structural parts of the interior are built before laying the deck planking so that the bigger pieces of wood and larger machinery can be more easily moved into and out of the hull.

# interior

It's near the end of the first year of construction. Snow and sleet sizzle against the tin roof of the Mugwump shed. Gusts pound fitfully against the walls. To look down into *Rebecca* from the staging around her deck is to suddenly see the schooner anew. In the fall, while the planking slowly revealed the shape of her hull, it also gradually closed off any view of the interior. If you climbed up over the rail in those days, you entered a space defined by a long, valentine-shaped procession of sawn and bent frames, sheathed and darkened by planking. It was like standing inside a giant wooden canoe.

But walk the scaffold along the hull today and the interior is transformed. The nature of the schooner reveals itself, for the first time, in structural and personal terms. Walls, called bulkheads, define the principal living and working quarters within the hull. Beginning at the stern and walking forward, there is a cabin for *Rebecca*'s professional captain and mate (known as the doghouse), which will also contain a navigation table and instruments; a stair leading down to the owner's stateroom, with a wide bunk on the port side and locker to starboard; the galley; the saloon, with seats and bunks lying along the hull; and the forecastle tucked into the bow, where before too long the owner's guests should hear the current gurgling by the waterline as they drift off to sleep in their bunks.

The saloon glows in the work lights hanging from the bulkheads. It is frigid. Steam from the breath hangs in the air after exhaling. Nat wears a heavy Irish sweater and vest, and his hair curls out from beneath a green beret. He tests the placement of a cabin top beam, which will arch broadly across the saloon. Back in the days of lofting there were diagrams of every important line in the hull. For the interior there is only a drawing.

"All I did was a sketch," says Nat. "It's easier just to do the sketch, then come in here and juggle things around." Yet the only meaningful change between his drawing of the interior four years ago and the construction now is the relocation of the galley, from just forward of the saloon to just aft of it. Even so, the shift in all this weight – stove, sink, icebox, and cabinets full of plates and cutlery – won't affect the trim of the hull once *Rebecca* is afloat. "You're talking about a thirty-four-

DAY 304
Early November 1998: Work begins on the living spaces within the hull and carries on through early February.

In no other place are the sailor's terms for the parts of a boat quite so confusing to the layman as the interior: The floor is called the sole, the paneling along the inside of the framing is called the ceiling, and the ceiling is called the overhead.

△ Casson Kennedy builds a grate for the shower floor in the owner's head (bathroom).

▷ Brad Ives, who selected all the tropical hardwood timber used for *Rebecca*, sits atop a pile of angelique.

Daniel Feinstein,
a newcomer to the crew,
glues up a ladder that leads
from the forward deckhouse
down to the saloon.

The forecastle, a cozy living space in the bow of the schooner during construction, this photo, and a few days before launch, right. The silver balli paneling below the bunk gleams in new varnish as work continues. The mattresses on the bunks, right, are covered in the tartan of the Malcolm family, who purchase the schooner before construction ends.

ton boat," Nat says. "Moving a few pounds around isn't going to make much of a difference in the balance of the boat."

The interior wood is mostly familiar – silver balli bulkheads, cabinets, and settees; white oak deck beams. What's surprising, after so much heavy work outside the hull, is the new feeling of delicacy within it: the long, narrow rills in the beaded face of the bulkheads; the mahogany trim that frames the cabinet doors; the curved corners of the rims – called fiddles – that keep mattresses from sliding off the bunks and plates from crashing off the shelves whenever *Rebecca* heels in a strong blow.

In the master stateroom, Pat Cassidy reviews his work in a corner where the hull meets the deck. Pat, twenty-nine, has worked on *Rebecca* in stints, going back to the summer before, when the crew was setting the last of the steam-bent frames. Otherwise he works in his own small, traditional boatbuilding shop just up the road from the Gannon and Benjamin yard.

Playing off the seaman's contracted pronunciation of the word "forecastle" (foke-sull), David Stimson, after a meeting with Nat in which they discuss the design of a pair of bunks in this cabin, concludes by saying, "We'd better go back to the other guys, or fo'c's'l be talking about us."

△ For the first-time sailor, it takes only a few minutes under sail to realize that a hull responds to every gust and lull in the wind. Fiddles (or lips) border nearly every horizontal surface within a sailboat because without them, no plate or book or mattress would remain where it lay on a counter, table, or bunk.

▷ Looking forward from the galley a few days before launch, *Rebecca*'s saloon and forecastle glow with contrasting hues of new varnish. Books and artwork line the shelving in the saloon. In the galley, kettles, mugs, well-braced plates, and a few bottles of wine wait for the first meals to be served aboard the schooner.

All along the length of the schooner, the corner where deck and hull meet is particularly vulnerable to the compressive, upward loading of the rig. To reinforce this critical corner where the deck beams fasten to the double-sawn frames, Pat has built and fastened a set of hanging knees. The wood – it must be stout as well as naturally and sharply curved to follow the angle of the corner – comes from the root of a hackmatack tree in Maine.

Pat lifts a work light up to a hanging knee in the corner of the master stateroom. With his finger, he traces the sharp turn in the grain that reveals how the trunk curved nearly 90 degrees into its root. "That's the whole reason to use a crook here," he says, "because the grain follows the curve, and that adds strength."

Pat is the most experienced young boatbuilder at Mugwump. He likes the way Gannon and Benjamin combines skilled boatbuilders with apprentices on a crew. The newcomers learn from master builders in the real world. And they help keep things moving along at a reasonable price.

"You don't want to be too top-heavy with skilled labor," he says, "and you don't want to have too many unskilled. You have Ted and Casson on the job so you can just get things done. You can't have thirty-dollar-an-hour guys making butt blocks. You need those lower-priced guys just to make it affordable. And you have to make it affordable or else none of these boats would ever get built."

At the bow, in the forecastle, John Armstrong, a former Coast Guardsman and now boatyard worker, sands a bulkhead, readying it for varnish. He likes to work on virgin wood. "I don't have to strip off eight coats of varnish to get to it," he says. "There are no water stains. No gouges anywhere."

But varnishing even new wood is a long, arduous endeavor of application and removal, of seeing progress and then willfully obliterating it, only to start all over again. Between each of the two base coats of sealer, as well as each of the five or six finish coats of varnish to come, John will sand every surface to rid it of blemishes endemic to the grain or caused by a machine or tool. "Varnish brings out the imperfections," he says.

The undoing of what's just been done doesn't end there. He must also vacuum and tack-cloth everything after each sanding because varnish abhors dust. With each coat, he uses increasingly fine grits of sandpaper. "The wood accepts the next coat that much more. And it helps me see where I've been and where I've got to go yet. If I don't knock enough gloss off, I get lost where I am. A lot of people say you can let your mind go to Jamaica while you sand and varnish. But you have to watch what you're doing. You spend a lot of time prepping it. You get your reward when the varnish goes on."

John likes to varnish when there's no one else working in the interior because that keeps down the dust.

What he doesn't know on this stormy afternoon is that work on the schooner *Rebecca* is about to stop for a very long time.

# *an unwelcome respite…*

## DAY 400

February 1998: Work on the schooner stops and the doors to Mugwump are padlocked for most of the next twenty-one months. During that time, the *Rebecca* project enters bankruptcy court and the boat's fate is unknown.

In the first week of February, the company Dan Adams established more than a year earlier to build the schooner – and through which he is officially financing the project – runs out of money. Nat and Ross have been concerned about Dan for months, watching as he falls further and further behind in his payments to vendors who supply the main boatyard with critical parts.

For Gannon and Benjamin – a company that has built its reputation on individual integrity and honesty and who is now receiving complaints from vendors – seeing this happen is a huge departure from their usual way of doing business.

Dan tries to parry the criticism, arguing that Nat and Ross have taken the schooner over budget – which both men vigorously deny. To the builders, Dan appears largely unconcerned about the impact this funding turmoil is having on the boatyard, and they now doubt his claim that he's reorganizing his finances and that the money will soon flow. The unanswered questions and unpaid bills are impacting on Nat and Ross's relationships with both their building crews and longtime suppliers. It is a critical moment in the boatyard's life, one Dan seems to ignore.

As the account runs dry in early February, both men wonder if Dan ever had the money to fully finance the boat, and construction stops. The machinery falls silent, the lights are turned off, and the Mugwump shed is filled with a gloomy, forbidding stillness.

Nat's immediate concern is finding new work for his crew. Todd and Casson join Pat Cassidy at his own shop in Vineyard Haven. Nat and Ted Okie migrate to the main yard, where construction has begun on the first substantial powerboat ever built by Gannon and Benjamin. David Stimson works on a few projects of his own. And with the hope that money will soon be found to resume work on *Rebecca*, Nat has John Armstrong sand and varnish her for just a few more days to take advantage of the unnatural, entirely dust-free quiet within the hull.

Finally, the work stops completely. As winter wears its cold way toward spring, most of the Mugwump tools are taken to the harborfront shop. The door is eventually padlocked. Inside is a schooner with her keel cut and ballasted, her hull framed and planked, her interior laid out but unfinished. In other yards, boats as far along as *Rebecca* have never found their way to the water, and so long as there is no money, the fate of this vessel lies somewhere between uncertainty and hope.

But not for Nat and Ross. Ross senses right away that the man who commissioned *Rebecca* has already lost her; the cost of the work ahead is just too high for someone who can't pay his suppliers now. Ross puts his faith in *Rebecca* herself. "From my point of view, the boat's got its own life," he says. "The boat's going to get finished." He's not sure who will take over proprietorship and complete the job, but he adds: "It won't sit without an owner for very long."

For most of the next twenty-one months, nothing happens at Mugwump. But a great deal happens within the federal bankruptcy system. More than a year after work stops, the company Dan Adams created to build the schooner files for bankruptcy protection. Then Dan files personally. Nat and Ross, watching all this, are angry and critical of Dan, a man they feel was not honest or upfront with them.

Neither of the bankruptcies startle Vineyarders – both Island newspapers follow the drama closely, and it's long been plain that the schooner's future depends on new ownership. But what surprises everyone is the place from which rescue suddenly comes: a couple from a village called Traquair, thirty miles south of Edinburgh, Scotland.

Brian and Pamela Malcolm know Martha's Vineyard because a family yacht, the forty-five-foot sloop *Josephine of Wight*, is being refit at Gannon and Benjamin. Pamela's family has long loved traditional sailing vessels – in the 1950s, her father built a twenty-five-foot wooden yacht in a family barn in the south of England – and with Brian about to retire from his partnership at an investment management firm in Edinburgh, the couple will soon have time to cruise wherever the winds take them. On a visit to the Island to check on the progress on *Josephine* in the spring of 2000, they visit the Mugwump shed, where little work has been done on the schooner for fourteen months. They find themselves captivated by *Rebecca* – her size, strength, beauty, and perhaps most deeply, her plight.

"It was this sudden spark that was ignited in both of us the moment we got on board," says Pamela. When Nat writes them in May to say that the schooner is for sale through the bankruptcy court, it takes the Malcolms only two days to decide to bid. In November 2000, the boat is theirs for $700,000. "It was just amazing how smoothly the whole thing went," says Brian. "That had to be a good omen. By early November, that was it, and the whole thing had taken less than six months – through the U.S. bankruptcy courts!"

Daniel Feinstein balances on the deck beams while he inspects a length of silver balli deck planking.

deck

Looking aft from the bow, the silver balli planking that will cover the forward deckhouse lies atop the deck beams.

# *deck*

After nearly two years in limbo, Mugwump and the schooner project come back to life. Only ten days after the Malcolms take official ownership – it's now the end of November 2000 – the lights are on, the tools are back, and Todd, Casson, Ted, and the more recent hire, Daniel Feinstein, rejoin Nat and David. A new sense of purpose and confidence fills the shed. "We're going to finish up the interior, we're going to be building deck hatches, companionways, finish laying the deck, doing general carpentry," says Nat. "We're going to finish up this American schooner for her new British owners."

It is a relief to everyone that Brian and Pamela Malcolm have fallen for *Rebecca* as they first saw her back in April. They plan to spend a season or two sailing up and down the East Coast and cruising the West Indies. At some point they expect to take *Rebecca* across the Atlantic to Ireland, the United Kingdom, and eventually the Mediterranean. With a skilled captain and mate, there are no temperate waters on the globe that this schooner will be unable to explore.

By February, the third winter since the keel was laid, there is a definite launching date: Tuesday, May 8, 2001, just three months ahead. But for the plumbing and the wiring, the interior is mostly finished, the varnish gleaming in the work lights. The hull has been sanded down and re-primed because the layoff of nearly two years has dried out her planking, despite the previous coat.

Work turns to the deck, where the deckhouses now stand fastened to the deck beams and carlins (another set of deck beams that runs fore and aft rather than from side to side). The deckhouses are built of teak, which has been seasoning for more than twenty years, bought from a man in Maine who never finished a boat project of his own. The forward deckhouse leads to a ladder down to the saloon, the larger deckhouse (or doghouse) aft to the professional crew's quarters, navigation area, and a private stairway to the owner's stateroom below. Todd is building the top over this deckhouse – a challenge because the crown gradually increases from nearly flat at the forward end of the deckhouse to a significant camber (or curve) aft. It's a project that tests his skills and often wakes him up with geometric puzzles to solve in the middle of the night.

**DAY 1058**
End of November 2000: Work resumes under the ownership of Brian and Pamela Malcolm.

For the plank-on-frame boatbuilder, the choice of wood is dictated by what's available for any given part: "If someone calls me up and says he's got a tree over here that'll do this or that, we'll get the tree and do it," says Nat. "It's a daily, hourly judgment call. If we're framing a deck, and we need a piece of wood with a certain sweep to it, we don't care if it's angelique or locust or white oak – it's finding the piece of wood."

△ David Stimson selects a deck plank from the stock of silver balli, which like the angelique in *Rebecca*'s keel and double-sawn frames is selected and milled from the rainforest.

▷ Silver balli, a long, straight-grained wood, is rich in oil and varnishes beautifully like teak, but is more plentiful and thus less expensive. Because it tolerates the frequent process of getting wet and drying out, silver balli is often used for planking hulls and decks, as it is in *Rebecca*.

The two deckhouses are in place, awaiting rectangular and round port lights (or windows). In the foreground, the deck planks have been fastened to the deck beams.

Todd, Nat, David, and Ted lift the cabin top gently onto the deckhouse; it lies perfectly atop the sides, rounding off the tall structure in a stately way. At that very moment, the appearance and character of the schooner somehow converge. With the addition of this cabin top, the spirit of the whole vessel suddenly locks itself directly into the great American schooner era of the 1930s – a heritage *Rebecca* will share from her rigging down to her ribs with General Patton's schooner, *When and If*, which now waits for her in the wintry quiet of Vineyard Haven Harbor.

All four men look at the doghouse cabin top for a few seconds. Nat turns to Todd. "Perfect, yeah," he says. "That's going to be outrageous looking." From the designer, no two sentences can carry greater praise.

Casson works on the companionway slide over the forward deckhouse – a movable cover built of wood that allows easier access down to the saloon. The camber, or curve, of this slide is slightly greater than the cabin top itself, and building it challenges Casson.

While building *Rebecca*'s deck, David Stimson also builds a small, light rowboat called a wherry. A master of wordplay, he tells the crew that it's the smallest one he's ever built of this type. He'll call it, he says, *The Least of My Wherries*.

He recalls his earliest days on the project – how he asked questions before he started work, how Nat and David advised him to let the work teach him as he went, and how right they were to advise it. "It's just a matter of getting experience," he says. "There's no real mystery about putting two pieces of wood together. You know you want the edges to be straight and they want to meet perfectly. There's no more questions to ask." "Casson has taken big steps," says Nat, reflecting on the progress made by the young builders on the *Rebecca* project. "He's very careful, very meticulous. When you ask him to do something, you don't have to worry about it being a half-assed job."

Ted Okie pays attention to his work and has grown more able. Todd McGee enjoys the challenges he's taken on and has sharpened skills that were admirable from the very start. But as the launch date for *Rebecca* approaches, Nat sometimes wonders how many of his young shipwrights will be able to stay in the traditional boatbuilding business on Martha's Vineyard for a lifetime, as he has.

Todd and Casson earn roughly a third of what they could make building houses – most of them houses that, at this point in their lives, neither young man can hope to buy. For both Todd and Casson, just holding on to a life on the Vineyard is the biggest challenge of all, one they measure paycheck to paycheck.

"It's hard to plan for your future," says Todd. He'd like to keep building wooden boats, but if he can't afford to do it on the Island, there aren't many other towns on the mainland where he might. Still, he likes being on the ocean, and he believes the Vineyard appreciates and supports its skilled craftsmen more than most other places do. "That's good," he says – though after a moment he adds, "but I don't know yet if it's enough to keep someone like me here or not."

The launch date of May 8, 2001, is firm – the Malcolms are flying from Scotland for it – and as spring approaches for the fourth time since *Rebecca*'s keel was laid, Mugwump begins to thrum with the excitement and urgency of a hard deadline, the first in the long saga of the schooner project.

But hard, sometimes tedious work remains.

The crew must finish laying and caulking the deck, begun just before the work stoppage. Deck beams of white oak arc across the hull; the shape gives the deck its camber, over which rain and seawater will sheet away through drains, called scuppers, in the bulwarks around the hull. Todd, Casson, and Ted fasten the deck planking – long strips of silver balli – to the deck beams. The fastening screws are bronze, dipped in a bedding compound to lubricate the screws as they are driven into the hard white-oak deck beams.

The deck is an area of special concern to plank-on-frame boatbuilders, says Ross. "Leaks through the deck are what lots of people find objectionable about a wooden boat. The bottom of the boat isn't hard to keep from leaking, because everything is put together so that it swells tightly against the piece next to it. But the deck sits up in the hot summer sun, and then you go for a sail and get it soaking wet. The wood expands and contracts, which can cause movement and gaps. Under certain conditions, even a very well built wooden boat is still going to pass some water somewhere." He reflects on the hundreds of pieces of wood in a traditional boat,

△ Once the planking is fastened to the deck, the crew uses wooden mallets to tap bungs (wooden plugs) over the screws to fill the holes.

▷ Kirsten Scott, to whom Ross proposes during the schooner project, knocks off the tops of the thousands of bungs in *Rebecca*'s deck.

Working at the bow and masked to keep the dust from his lungs, Todd McGee uses an orbital sander after the deck planking has been fastened and bunged on the schooner's deck. The sanding leaves a fine, dark powder round the sampson post, to which a line may be tied when the boat lies along a pier or on a mooring.

△ As with the planking in the hull, the grit must be dug from the seams in the deck after sanding so the planks can be caulked. The builders use a reefing hook to do this job – which in turn leaves more grit on the deck, and which must be vacuumed before the crew can caulk. Below, improvised kneepads provide welcome cushioning.

▷ Another round of caulking as mallet strikes iron and cotton is tucked into a deck seam.

The cotton used in caulking the deck comes in one-pound bundles and measures about an inch across. These are split and coiled into smaller bundles called hanks and tucked into the seams using a caulking iron and mallet. When the deck planking is fully caulked, *Rebecca* will have roughly two hundred pounds of cotton in her hull.

and the hundreds of joints where these pieces meet, all of which must be fastened and sealed together and made as watertight as possible. "It's a miracle to me," says Ross, "that these boats don't leak more than they do."

The deck is caulked the same way the hull was. But the strakes of silver balli in the deck are reedlike in comparison to those in the hull. Moreover, there are more than eighty of them across the deck amidships, and each seam must be caulked from bow to stern. For Mark, Todd, Casson, and Ted, it's another round of makeshift kneepads, of mallets ringing against caulking irons, necks crackling and shoulders popping from the effort and strain. During a break, Casson looks down the length of a seam he's tucking cotton into. Ted tells Casson he's skilled enough now to do the whole deck himself. Todd, sitting on his cabin top, smiles and says, "Be careful what you get good at."

At the end of the day, the crew climbs down the staging. Ted stops for a moment to dig at the dirt floor beneath the hull with his boot. Two inches down, he finds a patch of the plywood floor, gone lead-gray from the day when it was first painted white, with no trace of a pencil mark left upon it. He chuckles. "Lofting was a long time ago," he says, heading for the door.

Builders and Lacy, a
canine companion, take
a break on the staging
around the hull.

1 Pattern: A pattern for a bow roller, above left, which bears the weight and eases the raising and lowering of an anchor and its chain, and for a rudder hinge, above right. Gannon and Benjamin custom-designs and patterns many fittings for its boats and has them cast at the Mystic Valley Foundry. The finished products will be beautiful, functional, and long-lasting.

4 Molding sand: Arthur Anthony Sr., son of the founder of the yard, with a wheelbarrow full of molding sand, called Petrobond – a mixture of sand and petroleum that packs well and holds its shape when the pattern is removed.

5 Dusting:  Arthur Anthony Jr., grandson of the founder, applies a dusting of "parting powder" to ensure that the pattern can be removed easily, leaving behind a suitable mold. Given that molds vary in size and shape, the worker must use his expertise to ensure that the molten metal flows evenly into the mold and cools satisfactorily afterward.

# bronze

A sturdy wooden schooner requires sturdy bronze fittings, worthy of the hull and rig. Many of Rebecca's fittings are custom designed at the yard and cast at Mystic Valley Foundry in Somerville, Massachusetts – founded in 1936 and one of only a few foundries still doing this work in New England. It is dirty, dangerous work, requiring expertise and strength to do it properly.

**2** Ingot: A bronze ingot lies poised above the crucible (or container) in which it will be melted in a furnace. The melting temperature of bronze is about 1,900 degrees Fahrenheit, and the process of melting is called a "heat." At Mystic Valley, each crucible holds about two hundred pounds of molten metal.

**3** The "heat": With the "heat" well under way and the metal approaching the temperature at which it may be poured, various elements are added to the crucible to produce alloys useful for maritime fittings: silicone (which resists corrosion), magnesium (strong and corrosion-resistant), or aluminum (which adds toughness).

**6** Snagging: One of the most dangerous and unpleasant jobs at the foundry involves "snagging" a newly cast part – sanding or grinding away any excess bronze (which will be melted again and reused) without damaging the piece or injuring the worker.

**7** The finished product: Designed and patterned at Gannon and Benjamin and cast and finished at Mystic Valley Foundry, two custom-built cleats stand at the ready. Cleats are designed so that sailors may fasten lines (ropes) to them quickly and efficiently, whether lines from a pier to a deck or halyards and sheets that raise, lower, and control the sails. A line is looped in a crisscrossing pattern over the two ends of a cleat, with the last turn hitched (or twisted) to lock it in place.

# aloft

Dominic Zachorne sews leather around a mast hoop on the foremast of *Rebecca*. The luff (or forward part) of the foresail will be laced to these mast hoops, which are periodically coated with tallow to ease the raising and lowering of the sail and reduce the risk of chafing along the varnished mast.

A mockup of the mainmast, showing the interlocking design of Antonio Salguero's innovative bird's mouth technique. This trial run at the design allows Antonio to ensure that he accurately cuts the lip in the actual staves, which are used to build the masts.

# aloft

As work finally resumes at Mugwump in Vineyard Haven, construction of the two masts begins in Port Townsend, Washington, a seaport and paper-mill town at the entrance to Puget Sound.

The forces that act on the masts and hull of a sailboat are remarkably powerful. Through the wire rigging that holds the masts in place from the hull, these forces act like a bow and arrow, lifting up on the frames and planking, compressing the deck, and driving the base of the masts into the floor and keel timbers.

Despite these stresses, the wooden masts of a traditional boat must maintain their structure, flexibility, and strength through countless voyages, wind and sea conditions for years, and unexpected events. They must be built sturdily and rigged carefully to last.

The job of building *Rebecca*'s masts goes to Antonio Salguero, Ross's nephew, who runs Sound Boats, a one-man design and repair company on the Port Townsend waterfront.

Antonio, thirty-three, grew up in a coastal Connecticut town with his mother and two older sisters and spent summers, from the age of ten, with Ross in Vineyard Haven. For a time, they lived together on *Urchin*, Ross's cutter, and during his boyhood Antonio helped his uncle move and build houses. After Nat and Ross started the boatyard, Antonio worked there. He moved to Port Townsend after graduation from the naval architecture program at the Maine Maritime Academy in 1992.

Antonio shares Nat's and Ross's admiration for wooden boats, but the engineer in him likes to experiment a bit with traditional techniques when it appears to make sense. Nat has specified in his plans that he wants *Rebecca*'s masts to be hollow, which will reduce the weight aloft and lower the center of gravity in the boat so that she can carry more sail in a variety of winds. But the masts must also meet all the structural requirements for dependability over time, and that leaves open an important question: how to keep the mast timbers, called staves, from yielding to all the stresses on the masts and collapsing in on the core itself?

DAY 1107

Early January 2001: Work begins on the mainmast of *Rebecca* in Port Townsend, Washington.

When a boat with one mast – such as a sloop or cutter – sails close to the wind and heels over more than 30 degrees in a strong breeze, the compressive loading beneath the base of that mast can equal the entire weight of the boat.

△ Antonio Salguero sailed across the Atlantic after graduating from the naval architecture program at the Maine Maritime Academy. He then moved to Port Townsend, Washington, where he began to design and build boats on Puget Sound. Socket chisel in hand, he takes a momentary break from building *Rebecca*'s mainmast, five months before the schooner's launch. Below, a No. 5 bench plane, a favorite all-purpose plane for most traditional boatbuilders, used to round the edges of the staves after assembly.

The staves for *Rebecca*'s mainmast lie on a rack at the one-man shop where Antonio Salguero builds boats and spars. When finished, the two masts, measuring seventy-four and fifty-eight feet each, will be shipped across the country on a boat trailer.

# sails

THE MANUFACTURING PLANT where *Rebecca*'s sails are made is a vast steel building located in a small Maryland town on an island in the Chesapeake Bay. The sails are too big for Gretchen Snyder to build – that's the sailmaker's verb – in what is then her loft above the main shop at Gannon and Benjamin. Instead, the job goes to North Sails, by far the largest sail maker in the world, whose Stevensville facility will use the most advanced techniques to build a set of schooner sails whose basic configuration goes back well into the nineteenth century.

*Rebecca* will often carry four sails – a mainsail, foresail, forestaysail, and jib – and on days when the wind is light, a fifth called a fisherman, rigged high between the masts. The sail that will make

△ Building sails is now a science hurried along by computer designs and laser cutters. The only tools held over from the old days are the sewing machines that assemble sail panels – but of synthetic Dacron rather than cotton.

her rig look classic, even to the untrained eye, is the foresail. Four-sided, with a wooden spar angling upward from the foremast to hold its shape, the foresail will be gaff-rigged, which adds a bit more sail area, and thus more power, to a heavy cruising boat with a traditional schooner rig.

*Rebecca*'s sails will be built of Dacron, a general-purpose canvas that began to supplant cotton in the 1950s. "Cotton was miserable," says John Thompson, the designer in charge of the cut and assembly of *Rebecca*'s sails. "It would get wet and shrink, then dry and stretch. Dacron, to me, is pretty indestructible." But it's considered old-fashioned now, the canvas of choice for recreational sailors and low-tech, round-the-buoy racers. For North Sails, whose latest laminate sails of Kevlar and Mylar compete in the most demanding regattas in the world, Dacron is as close to tradition as the company ever gets.

In the center of the building lies the loft floor, paneled in plywood and painted blue. Here, not long ago, the designer knelt with shapes he'd drawn on paper, unrolled his canvas across the floor, refined dimensions and curves according to his experience and intuition, cut the sail panels with scissors, and assembled them by hand. Now it's computers, laser cutters, and the latest adhesives – the men and women on the floor following the design and directives of machines. Even *Rebecca*'s Dacron canvas will be put together this way.

The only step left over from the old days is the stitching together of the sail panels. Around the perimeter of the factory, a few women still sit at reliable old sewing machines, the Dacron crinkling as it slides under a whirring needle.

"We've gotten away from the traditional type of sail making," says John Thompson. "People who used to build sails on the floor were sailmakers; they sailed, they knew sails, they knew everything about them. There was a lot of crawling around on the ground, making marks, establishing curves, and everything else. This is like an automotive manufacturing facility. The guys put the parts together where the lines say to put them together. Sail making used to be an art. Now it's a science."

◁ Because *Rebecca*'s masts are so long, Antonio Salguero builds a twenty-foot, two-story extension to his shop to construct them. The wood for both spars is old-growth Sitka spruce from Canada and Washington State, the trees originally measuring somewhere between six and eight feet in diameter and standing between 150 and 200 feet tall.

North Sails identifies the sails it builds by the class of boat it builds them for. Since *Rebecca* is an original, custom design, the company calls her class a "Gannon and Benjamin 60" – the number referring to her length in feet on deck.

When Antonio wins the job – he matches the bid of an East Coast spar maker, including the additional cost to ship the masts across the country on a boat trailer – he tells Nat that to reinforce the staves around the core, he wants to use a "bird's mouth" technique, suggested to him by a Port Townsend boat designer and builder named Kit Africa. The method involves cutting a lip on the inside of each stave for the adjacent stave to lock itself against. At first Nat argues for building each mast in two halves, with wider and fewer staves, and gluing the halves together – a more established method.

"Nat said, 'I wouldn't do it that way, but go ahead if you want,'" says Antonio of the bird's-mouth technique. "I thought, 'Well, I'm putting a lot on the line here.' But Kit Africa said, 'Piece of cake. I'll walk you through all the steps, no problem.'"

From mills in Washington State and British Columbia, Antonio buys stocks of Sitka spruce – light, straight, flexible, and tolerant of the hundreds of cycles of

△ Systems of heavy pulleys, known to sailors as blocks, help adjust the running rigging of a sailboat, which involves the lines (or ropes) called halyards that raise and lower the sails, as well as other lines, called sheets, that control the angle they are set to the wind.

loading and non-loading that the masts must endure through the years. At its base, each mast measures at least ten inches in diameter, the foremast over fifty-eight feet long, and the mainmast just under seventy-four feet. Eight staves, built in sets, make up the structure of both masts, the hollow core forming an octagon.

In his shop at the Port Townsend Boat Haven, Antonio has glued and clamped together the staves in one section of the mainmast. They lie on a spar table, which is framed like any other table, but without a top so that a mast may be easily clamped and built. With long runs of a bench plane, Antonio rounds off the angled outer edges of the mast where the staves meet. Slivers of spruce, thin as mica, fall gently onto Cricket, his seven-year-old Australian shepherd, lying in a shaft of sunlight.

Having already built the foremast – it hangs from a rack over his head – Antonio is increasingly confident that the bird's-mouth technique will hold together as designed. But he recalls a morning of panic two weeks before, when he was gluing the foremast and discovered the plastic straps he was using to hold the staves together weren't strong enough to do the job.

"Epoxy being epoxy, with a finite cure time of about half an hour, it was like, 'Oh, shit,'" says Antonio. He ran to his van and sped to the boat shop of a former

As with the interior of the hull, varnishers of spars need a clean and controlled environment to keep grit from marring their work.

# rigging

Strung from the waterline and deck of the hull to the tops of the masts, Rebecca's wire rigging – some of it measuring half an inch in diameter – holds the two masts in place and bears the stresses produced by 1,750 square feet of canvas driving a sixty-foot, 76,000-pound schooner through every sea she will ever confront.

His hair is long, braided, and laced with leather ties. He's a licensed captain, sailor, boat-builder, rope maker, and builder and restorer of ship models. He's also *Rebecca*'s rigger. Dominic Zachorne of Wickford, Rhode Island, is a nineteenth-century man working in the most traditional of maritime trades two centuries later.

3 Serving: Now the wire is served with a marlin line that has been tarred. A wooden serving mallet keeps tension and uniformity in the wire.

4 Leathering: The wire is leathered to prevent chafing of the rig and to create a cushion where a spar or another part of the rigging may lie against it. The sailmaker's "palm" on his hand is an old tool used the same way as a tailor's thimble is today – to push the needle through the work.

**2** Parceling: Parceling smooths over wire with heavy canvas or cotton, which also absorbs the tar beneath it. This further protects the wire from the corrosive effects of weather and water.

**1** Tarring down the wire: The wire is tarred before worming (using line to lace the grooves between the strands) and parceling (wrapping) – three steps designed to create a barrier from the weather.

**5** Seizing: The beginning of a "seizing" on the throat of an eye splice (a loop in a wire or line aboard a boat). Seizing helps relieve the strain on the nearly completed eye.

**6** Rigging: Dominic, working with Todd McGee, sews leather around a mast hoop on *Rebecca*'s foremast. The luff (or forward edge) of the foresail is tied to the mast hoops, which help with raising and lowering the sail; the leather helps to prevent chafing along the varnished mast. Just to the right of the mast, and not yet attached, the gaff hangs from a block (or pulley). The uppermost part of the quadrilateral foresail is lashed to the gaff, which gives shape to a sail whose design helps add extra power in a schooner rig.

The main boom of the schooner, to which the bottom of the mainsail is lashed: The bronze fitting around the end is the clew iron, a fabricated bronze ring that fastens the lowest, outermost corner of the sail to the boom. The boom itself is hollow, like the masts, to save weight and is built of four staves of Douglas fir. The boom is blocked at both ends to help fill and reinforce the core.

△ Antonio Salguero's Australian shepherd Cricket long ago learned to live with the detritus of the boatbuilding and spar-making trade.

employer, who was on a morning coffee break with his crew. "I came running in and said, 'I need spar clamps! Now!'"

The employer and his crew had heard about the bird's-mouth technique Antonio was using and guessed his predicament. They took a minute to chortle over the kinds of trouble traditional builders get themselves into when they go apostate in their methods, then pointed to the locker where the spar clamps were hanging.

"But they were fit so tightly it took me five minutes just to get them out of there," says Antonio. "They were like a Chinese puzzle, interlocked. I'm yanking these things out, cursing. Grabbed what I could carry in two armloads. Threw them in my van. Raced back. Gave them to the guys who were slathering glue. Ran back for another load."

He stops planing the staves for a moment and looks out the window, shaking his head and smiling at the humor of his fellow boatbuilders. "More chuckles," he says of his desperate return trip to their shop. "Humble pie."

launch

With the Reverend Woody Bowman by her side, Pamela Malcolm, wearing the family tartan, expresses delight as a bottle of Champagne showers the newly christened schooner *Rebecca of Vineyard Haven*.

Maynard Silva, a legendary Vineyard guitarist, harmonica player, and bluesman, works part time as a sign painter. At Mugwump, he paints *Rebecca*'s name and homeport on the transom, the face of the schooner's stern.

# *launch*

One day before launch, *Rebecca* gets a longer name. From the days when Nat Benjamin first drew her lines almost six years before, the plan was for the schooner to go in the water with the name "Rebecca" painted on her stern, and the homeport of Vineyard Haven below it. Pamela and Brian Malcolm, her new owners, love the name – for them it evokes the Cornish coastline of the Daphne du Maurier novel – and especially the idea that the homeport will tie her to the harbor and boatyard where she was designed and built.

But as citizens of the United Kingdom they cannot claim an American harbor as her home. So overnight the schooner is legally designated a British vessel. At the first opportunity, the name on her transom will be expanded to read "Rebecca of Vineyard Haven" and her homeport Cowes, on the Isle of Wight, from which Pamela's family has sailed for many years.

The late afternoon of Tuesday, May 8, 2001, is sunny, with a summery southwest breeze ruffling the surface of the harbor. More than four hundred people fill the lot at the Tisbury Marine Railway Company, where *Rebecca* and her hydraulic trailer rest on a pair of rail cars whose rusty track slopes down to a rising tide in the harbor. At four o'clock, Nat stands before a microphone. He thanks Pamela and Brian for seeing the schooner through to a degree of fit and finish "beyond our wildest dreams." Speaking for Ross as well as himself, Nat salutes the crew – "an exceptional collection of unusual vagabonds and renegades" – who with humor, spirit, skill, and devotion "put so much into the boat."

Wrapped in cloth and tied up with red ribbon, a bottle of Champagne hangs from the bow. At 4:10, after a blessing by the Reverend Woody Bowman, Pamela, who wears the Malcolm tartan on a sash, pulls back on the bottle and lets it crash into the bronze bobstay fitting on the stem. With bouquets filling her cockpit, dress flags rigged over short, temporary masts from bow to stern, and the blue and white St. Andrew's Cross – the national flag of Scotland – waving easily from her stern, the schooner begins to rumble slowly backward toward the harbor.

At 4:25, with the rail cars submerged but the hull still supported just above the water by the trailer, the hydraulic arms on the rear car drop suddenly, and the stern

DAY 1220

Early May 2001: Schooner *Rebecca of Vineyard Haven* is launched before a crowd of four hundred Vineyarders at the Tisbury Marine Railway Company in Vineyard Haven.

To ensure the bottle of Cuvée Dom Pérignon 1992 breaks when it strikes the bobstay fitting, Nat scours the bottle with a glass cutter. "That should do it," he says after twenty cuts – at which point the bottle breaks in his hands. Brad Ives scurries home and retrieves another bottle from his recent wedding. Before the Malcolms arrive, it is secretly wrapped in the cloth as a substitute. Whatever variety or vintage of Champagne actually christens *Rebecca*, Brad says later, it wasn't Cuvée Dom Pérignon 1992.

While *Rebecca* begins to cruise the Atlantic coastline, it's possible that the Gannon and Benjamin boat that travels farther than any other is also one of its smallest: a dinghy that serves as a tender to *Zorra*, above, a seventy-two-foot yawl restored by the boatyard after a fire in Norfolk, Virginia, in 1986.

▷ The wineglass shape of *Rebecca*'s newly finished hull, still surrounded by staging, fills the Mugwump shed on the morning she is towed to the Vineyard Haven Harbor launch site. Wooden timbers and wedges still support the schooner, while the retracted hydraulic arms of the trailer stand ready to balance her hull.

With traffic inching along on the far side of the trailer, *Rebecca*, her hull high and handsome in the morning sunlight, backs down Beach Road to the launch site.

In celebration of *Rebecca*'s owners' Scottish heritage, Tony Peak of Vineyard Haven pipes the schooner to the launch site.

△ A formal invitation to *Rebecca*'s launch is sent to hundreds of Islanders, but the event itself draws the attention of the whole harbor. *Rebecca* is launched under the thundering fire of three cannons emplaced around the shoreline, a flyby by a Korean War-era warbird trailing white smoke, and jets of water arcing from the stern of an incoming ferry.

△ Ross Gannon's mother Janie and his twins Olin and Greta, passengers in a home-designed wicker pram, follow *Rebecca* across Beach Road to the site of her launch at the Tisbury Marine Railway Company in Vineyard Haven.

thumps into the harbor with a splash and a cheer from the crowd. At that moment, cannons fire from three wharves around the waterfront. The ferry *Nantucket*, gliding into Vineyard Haven, whistles a long blast, and crewmen with fire hoses at her stern door send two jets of water arcing into the sunlight. A single-engine Navy aircraft, a veteran of the Korean War, rockets over the schooner, trailing white smoke. From *Rebecca*'s stern, Casson and Todd throw lines to waiting powerboats. As her bow creases the water, the boats pull, and the new schooner drifts back from her trailer.

It has taken forty-one months, two owners, and hundreds of days of uncertainty, but now the largest sailing vessel built on Martha's Vineyard in one-hundred forty-one years has finally been christened and launched.

*Rebecca of Vineyard Haven* is afloat.

She is towed to a pier neighboring the Gannon and Benjamin Marine Railway. On the beach where, in the summer of 1978, Nat and Ross steam-bent new frames for *Urchin* and decided within the space of two days to open a boatyard for the men and women of Vineyard Haven who desperately needed help caring for their

Though the waterline was painted earlier to establish a clean, sharp line below the white paint on the hull, most of *Rebecca*'s bottom is painted by Todd McGee only a day before launch. The hydraulic arms supporting the hull are lowered just long enough for him to apply the bottom paint as he reaches it.

The ferry *Martha's Vineyard*
glides by the topsail schooner
*Shenandoah* a few minutes
after six on the morning of
*Rebecca*'s launch.

old wooden boats, a crowd gathers to celebrate the launch of their newest and grandest vessel. There is traditional Irish music and a picnic of shish kebabs and hamburgers prepared by The Black Dog Restaurant.

But to Brian Malcolm's surprise, few people seem interested in eating as the party gets under way. Many stand in a line on the pier, waiting for the chance to board *Rebecca*, which nods easily against the wharf, her bow pointing northeast, toward open water.

Two months of work remain before *Rebecca* first sails. There is more varnish to lay on throughout the interior, a fuel line to repair after her first short excursion under power, and equipment to load, from anchor chain to dinnerware.

In the meantime, the planking in the hull begins to swell in the salt water of Vineyard Haven Harbor, further compressing the seams the crew caulked nearly three years earlier. In the first hours after launch, about four inches of water seep through the hull into *Rebecca*'s bilge, a volume everyone expected and that was easily managed by running her pumps every few hours. A few days later, the pumps run just two or three times during the day, and for only a few minutes at a time.

On deck, it's a different story. Nat and the crew discover that they will have to re-putty as much as a quarter of the deck planking: The putty they used back when they were sealing the deck has, in many places, failed to adhere. But to the builders,

▽ Dress flags flying, *Rebecca* pauses momentarily over Vineyard Haven Harbor as her cradle, supported by cars on the marine railway, edges stern-first into the water.

Pam Benjamin and Brian Malcolm, above, aboard Rebecca after her launch. Ross Gannon and Nat Benjamin, above right, with their mothers, Janie Gannon and Joan Ellett, enjoy a moment in Rebecca's cockpit after the launch.

digging out the defective sealer and doing part of the job again is a manageable problem, the sort of thing they expect to happen somewhere either on, or in, a boat as she transitions from shed to water and construction to a life under sail. No big deal, says Todd as he re-putties part of the deck under a blue sky, and he laughs: "It's not like it's a new product from Chrysler."

In late May, the hollow, round masts arrive on a boat trailer from Port Townsend, Washington, and final coats of varnish are brushed on. Over the Fourth of July holiday, Dominic Zachorne sails to Vineyard Haven from the family shop in Wickford, Rhode Island. With Nat and a crew, Dominic lifts the masts onto a set of dollies and walks them from Mugwump down Beach Road to the Tisbury Wharf Company, an industrial lot on the Vineyard Haven waterfront where *Rebecca*'s tropical hardwoods were first stacked when they arrived from Suriname.

One after the other, a crane lifts the foremast, then the mainmast, each one turning lazily as it rises high over the hull. The men take hold of the base and slide it through the deck, lowering each mast in turn onto its foundation, called a mast step. The foremast step lies across five floor timbers, the mainmast four. The two mast steps will help diffuse the fearsome compressive loading that the masts and rigging will inflict on the keel timber when *Rebecca* heels over in a strong breeze.

For the rest of the day, Dominic supervises the splicing, fastening, and tuning of the stays and shrouds. From every point along the shoreline, *Rebecca*'s masts add two new landmarks to the harbor, further defining Vineyard Haven as a place where plank-on-frame boats are built, maintained, and sailed.

*Rebecca* is now just eight days away from her own maiden voyage.

On the day of that first sail, the breeze comes around the headland of West Chop from the west, steady and mild. The first course *Rebecca* ever sails is known as a reach, with the wind blowing directly across the hull from the port (or left) side, her four principal sails full and angled some 45 degrees off the starboard (or

The founding partners of the Gannon and Benjamin Marine Railway. Across the harbor, *When and If*, an inspiration for much of *Rebecca*'s design and construction, wears dress flags to celebrate the launch of a new, but still traditional, wooden schooner.

Nat helps steady *Rebecca*'s foremast and Dominic Zachorne sorts the rigging as a crane holds it aloft over *Rebecca*'s deck. Stepping (or setting) both masts takes three hours, and most of the rigging is finished before sundown. In a week and a day, the schooner will be ready for her first sail. Using a spar dolly, right, *Rebecca*'s mainmast is wheeled down Beach Road to the schooner.

right) side. She leaves Vineyard Haven astern, pointing for Falmouth Heights on Cape Cod, three miles across Vineyard Sound. Aboard the schooner are Pamela and Brian and several family members, Todd and Casson, Brad and Dominic, her captain Tony Higgins, Nat and Ross.

There is talk and laughter sixty feet aft in the cockpit, but what you hear at the bow – with the forestaysail and jib curving away from the deck in a great, forward-driving tandem of canvas – is the periodic sighing of the bow wave below your feet, the tiny whistle of the breeze through the forestay, and silence from the schooner herself. No rumble or whine from an engine below, no creak from the rigging above. Just a rhythmic, organic *whump-hiss* as her wooden stem rises and falls through the easy Vineyard Sound chop.

The sails are pulled in closer, Pamela turns the wheel a few degrees to port, and the schooner's bow swings left across the distant shoreline, pointing more to the west, toward the distant lighthouse at Nobska Point. *Rebecca*'s sailing closer to the wind now, heeling more, the spray flying further off her bow.

In the silence of hull and rig, you feel how eager *Rebecca* is to keep lifting herself toward the direction of the wind. Twenty minutes into her first cruise, everything that Nat drew at his table and built with his colleagues into her hull feels wholly alive, perfectly balanced, and eager to fly. As she clears the point at West Chop, the breeze strengthens, *Rebecca* shoulders herself down into the sea, urges herself ahead, and you take hold of the forestay and think about something Ross said right before she was launched:

"Boats are like poetry. They are an incredibly interesting way to travel. Boats are functional art. They require both science and art together to work well. That is what makes them so interesting and worthwhile."

"It's always a big learning curve as you go along here – all sorts of stuff that you don't think of at the drawing board that come up once you're building it. And of course you have an idea – but you don't really know – how it's going to sail until you haul the sails and cast off. And so that's always very exciting. It's always a thrill to sail a boat for the first time. It's a surprise."

— NAT BENJAMIN

"The most exciting adventure
of our lives had begun."

PAMELA MALCOLM
*upon the purchase of* Rebecca

IN THE NINE YEARS since her launch, *Rebecca of Vineyard Haven* fulfills all the promises drawn in her lines and built into her hull as a traditional cruising schooner. She's tough, speedy, easily handled, spacious, and comfortable above decks and below. She takes to every sea over which she sails as if she were designed just for those waters. Most important, she's obviously great fun to sail, given the distance she travels and the places she goes.

With her owners and crew, she sails the East Coast to Maine twice, visits Bermuda, and explores the Caribbean twice (the British Virgin Islands, the Grenadines). She makes a trans-Atlantic passage to Ireland and then on to Great Britain. She sails across the English Channel to northern France, along the coastlines of Spain and Portugal. She enters the Straits of Gibraltar and spends three summers cruising the Mediterranean from Cannes to the Balearics, Corsica, Sardinia, and the west coast of Italy.

And fast?

Within a year of her launch, *Rebecca* wins two prestigious classic yacht races – the Sweethearts of the Caribbean Regatta in Tortola as well as her own class at the Antigua Classics Yacht Regatta. She also competes three times in the Régate Royale at Cannes.

And in the summer of 2004, at her home port in Cowes, *Rebecca of Vineyard Haven* competes in the prestigious British Classic Yacht Club Annual Regatta and wins the Je Ne Sais Quoi Trophy, awarded to that yacht felt by the judges to be "the most stunning, the most elegant, the most hospitable, and most in keeping with the theme."

TIM WRIGHT

# afterword

DURING THE EARLY 1970s, Martha's Vineyard's main port of entry consisted of a casual mix of commercial and residential activity and a colorful group of enthusiastic sailing and boating enthusiasts. Unlike so many vacation destinations, Vineyard Haven Harbor, with its affordable moorings, was accessible to the people of the town. Standing tall in the anchorage, the 108-foot topsail schooner *Shenandoah* loomed over the fleet, her raking masts and sleek clipper hull a beacon of nineteenth-century maritime authenticity. It was a laid back, understated, quaintly disorganized, and pleasantly unpretentious place.

Not a whole lot has changed since then – just more boats.

But something else was stirring in these waters. A handful of knowledgeable watermen and local citizens had serendipitously organized a seaport that encouraged a traditional working waterfront while the rest of America's coastwise trades were being systematically dissolved and replaced with oversized, opulent developments pandering exclusively to corporate America at leisure. Thanks to these visionary individuals who fought to preserve the shipyards, docks, commerce, and ecology, this year-round vitality continues to thrive today.

Ross and I quietly inquired in 1979 about setting up a wooden boatbuilding and repair facility. For the most part, we were welcomed and encouraged. Concurrently, an Island-wide, nationally publicized groundswell of opposition to a proposed McDonald's hamburger franchise successfully thwarted the Golden Arches' effort to establish a foothold on Martha's Vineyard. We rode in on the victory slipstream, landing on the very beach where the fryolators were intended to envelop potatoes in hot grease.

Despite the questionable sanity of creating a nineteenth-century wooden boat business as the rest of the world was rushing into the "no maintenance" mantra of the twenty-first, we plowed ahead. The work was stimulating and challenging, though the hours were long. As we cultivated relationships with some of New England's eclectic collection of deteriorating classic yachts and their often eccentric owners, a symbiosis evolved. We would provide them with a vessel that would stay afloat, and they gave us much-needed job security. We gained more skills and confidence and soon realized that the mystique associated with building new traditional yachts was mostly "myst," so new custom designs and construction became a large part of our annual repertoire.

There were a few bumps in the road, as in any worthwhile endeavor, but jumping hurdles made us smarter and added a dash of humility to our disposition, which is always a good growth hormone.

By the time we closed in on our first decade in business, we had settled into a comfortable backlog of steady employment, a modest but predictable financial forecast, a company reputation beyond reproach, and just possibly a hint of hubris within the deeper psyche.

The wake-up call came around midnight, October 17, 1989, when the boatyard was engulfed in a blazing inferno, and everything we had worked so

△ Two of the largest boats ever designed and built by Gannon and Benjamin – *Rebecca*, on the left, and *Juno* – share a moment under Vineyard skies.

hard to achieve vanished before us in nature's terrifying furnace. The devastation was numbing, and the future full of doubt.

Returning, dazed, to the worksite the next morning, we were greeted by dozens of stunned but determined individuals, their bodies hunched over in blackened clothing, bare hands digging through the rubble for tools, hardware, personal belongings, anything salvageable. Although we were unaware of it at the time, this dismal gray morning was the beginning of a new wave of our waterfront enterprise. We had crossed the Rubicon of uncertainty and were now propelled forward by the energy and goodwill of the Island community and beyond. The message was clear: rebuild the boatyard and get back to work. This cathartic event sealed our connection with our Island as decisively as when a spectator resolves to become a player.

Building the schooner *Rebecca* was another transformative phase in our brief history on the waterfront. Initial machinations notwithstanding, the vessel was completed on budget and has brought great pleasure to her owners and to the numerous guests who have sailed aboard. The sixty-foot *Rebecca* was soon followed by the sixty-five-foot schooner Juno. Keeping track of these grand vessels as they sail the world's oceans is a source of great satisfaction. But the level of fulfillment is not a condition of the magnitude of the project but rather the nurturing of the soul. It is helping a grandson learn to row, guiding an apprentice spiling a plank, raising sail on a voyage outward bound, coaching a young sailor at the helm – enjoying the whole spectrum of life and witnessing beauty in a broken world.

We hope you felt both the joy and the beauty in the pages of this book.

*Nat Benjamin*

# 3o years:
Nat Benjamin and Ross Gannon can look across Vineyard Haven Harbor and see the work of two lifetimes sailing before their eyes. Some of the boats they've restored go back a century. Some they've built new will sail for a century more. Here's the record of the new boats that have come out of this traditional Vineyard boatyard on its thirtieth anniversary:

△ A skiff, newly repaired by the boatyard, is ready to go back to work in January 2010.

SWALLOWS & AMAZONS

LIBERTY

CHARLOTTE

| # | DATE | NAME | DESCRIPTION | DESIGNER | FIRST OWNER |
|---|---|---|---|---|---|
| 1 | 1980 | Sally May | Canvasback, 25' c/b/ sloop | Nat Benjamin | J. Taylor |
| 2 | 1981 | Meta (now Seasons) | 20' catboat | Nat Benjamin | C. Sullivan* |
| 3 | 1982 | Patita | Canvasback II | Nat Benjamin | W. Warick* |
| 4 | 1984 | Speeding Duck | Canvasback III | Nat Benjamin | M. Wheeler |
| 5 | 1985 | Swallows and Amazons | Cygnet, 23' gaff sloop | Nat Benjamin | J. Evans* |
| 6 | 1986 | Liberty | 40' gaff sloop | Nat Benjamin | P. Lombardi* |
| 7 | 1986 | Zorra's tender | 12' Cats Paw | Joel White | G&B* |
| 8–11 | 1987 | 4 Baby Bens | 10' yacht tender | Nat Benjamin | |
| 12 | 1988 | Lana and Harley (now Calabash) | 44' gaff schooner | Nat Benjamin | Y. Yamamoto* |
| 13 | 1990 | Encore | 37.5' gaff ketch | Nat Benjamin | A. Kent* |
| 14 | 1991 | Candle in the Wind (now Eliza) | 30' gaff yawl | Nat Benjamin | N. Verey* |
| 15 | 1991 | 12' pond boat | skiff, sailing dinghy | Nat Benjamin | A. Fisher* |
| 16 | 1995 | Tern | Tern, 28' gaff yawl | Nat Benjamin | W. Diver* |
| 17–19 | 1995 | 3 Periwinkles | 11' Periwinkle | Nat Benjamin | Sail MV |
| 20 | 1996 | Maybe Baby (now Nell) | 24' k/cb gaff sloop | Nat Benjamin | W. Graham* |
| 21 | 1996 | —————— | 12' yacht tender | Nat Benjamin | L. Stix |
| 22 | 1997 | Willy Winship | 16' sailing skiff | John Atkin | R. Olsen |
| 23 | 1997 | Blue Rhythm | Bella, 21' gaff sloop | Nat Benjamin | H. Begle |
| 24 | 1998 | Quitsa | Quitsa, 14' gaff sloop | Nat Benjamin | J. Kenney* |
| 25 | 1998 | Rosalee | Bella II | Nat Benjamin | D. McCullough |
| 26 | 1998 | Hermes | 11' yacht tender | Nat Benjamin | C. Evan |
| 27 | 1999 | Daybreak | Bella III | Nat Benjamin | S. Corkery |
| 28 | 1999 | Little Love | 12' skiff | Ross Gannon | D. Driscoll |
| 29 | 1999 | Isabella | Bella IV | Nat Benjamin | Stout & Butler |
| 30 | 1999 | Elisa Lee | 32' power boat | Nat Benjamin | J. Edwards* |
| 31 | 2000 | Relemar | Dory | Nat Benjamin | M. Tempelsman |
| 32 | 2000 | Black Rose | Tern, 28' gaff yawl | Nat Benjamin | K. Bonstrom |
| 33 | 2000 | On Gordons Pond | 11' yacht tender | Nat Benjamin | |
| 34 | 2001 | Rebecca | 60' auxiliary schooner | Nat Benjamin | B. Malcolm |
| 35 | 2001 | Hope | Tern, 28' gaff yawl | Nat Benjamin | R. Doyle |
| 36 | 2001 | Wonder | Tern, 28' gaff yawl | Nat Benjamin | A. Senchak |
| 37 | 2002 | Slipper | 31' gaff yawl | Nat Benjamin | B. Dwyer* |

MAYBE
BABY

| # | DATE | NAME | DESCRIPTION | DESIGNER | FIRST OWNER |
|---|------|------|-------------|----------|-------------|
| 38 | 2003 | Celeste | 28' k/cb gaff sloop | Nat Benjamin | B. Crosby |
| 39 | 2003 | Faith | Quitsa II | Nat Benjamin | C. Linneman |
| 40 | 2003 | Cygnet | Quitsa III | Nat Benjamin | D. Ogilvie |
| 41 | 2003 | Zerviah | Bella V | Nat Benjamin | R. Rudick |
| 42 | 2003 | Sparrow | Bella VI | Nat Benjamin | D. Pesch |
| 43 | 2003 | Oscar | 8' dinghy | Oscar Pease | MV Museum |
| 44 | 2003 | Juno | 65' auxiliary schooner | Nat Benjamin | R. Soros |
| 45 | 2004 | Epiphany | Buzzards Bay 25 | N.G. Herreshoff | J. Wolosoff |
| 46 | 2004 | Juno tender | 11' tender | Nat Benjamin | R. Soros |
| 47 | 2005 | Ilona | 29' Bass Boat | Nat Benjamin | C. Klinck |
| 48 | 2005 | Advent | 26' Alerion | N.G. Herreshoff | R. Hearn |
| 49 | 2005 | Little Wonder | 11' tender | Nat Benjamin | A. Senchak |
| 50 | 2005 | Ark Royale II | 16' Whitehall | John Gardener | B. Hall |
| 51 | 2005 | Zephyr | 22' Sharpie | J. Naimark-Rowse | J. Rowse |
| 52 | 2006 | Here and Now | 38' sloop | Nat Benjamin | M. Warburg |
| 53 | 2006 | Quatorze | 21' Runabout | Nat Benjamin | D. Campbell |
| 54 | 2006 | Basta | 10' tender (H&N) | Nat Benjamin | M. Warburg |
| 55 | 2007 | Alliance | 32' Bass Boat | Nat Benjamin | M. Cook |
| 56 | 2007 | Alliance tender | 11' tender | Nat Benjamin | M. Cook |
| 57 | 2007 | Zerviah tender | 11' tender | Nat Benjamin | R. Rudick |
| 58 | 2007 | Charlotte | 50' auxiliary schooner | Nat Benjamin | N. Benjamin |
| 59 | 2007 | Peapod | 16' Peapod | John Gardener | S. Goodick |
| 60 | 2008 | Jono | 14' pond boat | Nat Benjamin | G. Thomas |
| 61 | 2008 | Sophia | 11' tender to Eliza | Nat Benjamin | H. Fish |
| 62 | 2008 | Christine | 24' catboat | Nat Benjamin | D. Mitchell |
| 63 | 2009 | Calypso | 15' dory | Nat Benjamin | D. Kline |
| 64 | 2009 | Neighborhood Bully | 36' power yacht | Nat Benjamin | J. Weber |
| 65 | 2009 | Sheena (now Wave) | Holmes Hole 29 | Nat Benjamin | C. Linneman, G&B* |
| 66 | 2009 | Belle | 9'4" yacht tender | Nat Benjamin | J. Forsgren |
| 67 | 2009 | _____ | 9'4" Legend yacht tender | Nat Benjamin | T. Mullins |
| 68 | 2010 | Naima | 28' k/cb Marconi sloop | Nat Benjamin | W. Ryan |
| 69 | 2010 | _____ | 44' sloop | Antonio Salguero | R. Gannon |

\* Since sold to another owner

HERE & NOW

TERN

BLUE RHYTHM

CELESTE

# glossary

**Aft**: at, toward, or near the stern (or back) of a boat.

**Aloft**: overhead, above, or up in a mast.

**At sea**: on the ocean or during a voyage.

**Backbone**: a synonym for keel.

**Ballast keel**: that part of the keel, cast in lead, which adds weight.

**Ballast-to-displacement ratio**: the percentage of a boat's total weight to be found in its keel.

**Batten**: a thin, flexible strip of wood used to shape and measure lines during lofting. Also, a length of wood or plastic slid into the leech (or back edge) of a sail to reinforce it.

**Bilge**: the lowest part of the interior of a hull.

**Bilge stringer**: a length of timbers that reinforces the inside of the frames along the area of the waterline.

**Bobstay fitting**: on a boat with a bowsprit (a spar that extends forward from the bow), the chain from there down to the stem at the waterline. The bobstay counteracts stress on the forestay.

**Body plan**: in the design, a view of the bow and stern of the boat, as seen head-on.

**Boom**: on boats with a fore-and-aft (or bow-to-stern) rig, the spar to which the bottom of a sail attaches.

**Bowsprit**: the spar extending forward from the bow to which the forestay is attached.

**Bulkhead**: a wall or partition aboard a boat.

**Bulwark**: a solid railing around a deck.

**Bung**: a cylindrical cap of wood that covers the head of a screw in a deck or hull plank.

**Camber**: a curve in a deck or covering from the center to the sides.

**Ceiling**: an interior wall, attached to the frames, that helps to reinforce them.

**Chain locker**: a forward compartment where the anchor and gear are stowed.

**Chainplate**: a metal fitting at the side of a boat to which the shrouds (a set of rigging wires) are fastened.

**Covering board**: the wide, outermost plank in a deck.

**Cradle**: A wooden framework on which a boat is placed on land for maintenance or repair.

**Cross spawl**: a plank set across a hull to help reinforce frames once they have been set up on the keel.

**Cutter**: a single-masted sailboat, its mast set farther aft (or back) than a sloop, and carrying two headsails.

**Deadwood**: the heavy pieces of wood below the keel timber and behind the ballast keel that make up the structure of the keel as a whole.

**Deck beam**: A timber that runs across the hull from side to side and supports the deck planking.

**Displacement**: the weight of a boat as measured by the weight of the water displaced by the hull.

**Draft**: the minimum depth of water a vessel needs to float.

**Eye splice**: a loop permanently woven into a line (rope) or wire.

**Fair**: to adjust lines in a design, align timbers during construction, or make smooth those parts of the structure or surface of a hull that are rough.

**Fiddle**: a lip or rail at the edge of a table or counter to prevent items from sliding off.

**Fin keel**: a slender, narrow keel found on many modern sailboats.

**Floor timber**: a structural piece fastened across the keel timber to which the bases of the frames are fastened.

**Fore**: anything forward on a vessel; the opposite of aft.

**Fore-and-aft**: a type of sailboat rig in which the sails are arrayed along the centerline of a boat.

**Forecastle (or fo'c's'l)**: a living space within the bow of a boat.

**Forekeel**: the timber that gives structural shape and strength to the bow.

**Foremast**: on a two-masted schooner rig, the first of the two masts.

**Foresail**: on a two-masted schooner, the sail rigged to the foremast.

**Forestay**: a wire that supports a mast from the bow and from which a forestaysail may be rigged.

**Forestaysail**: the sail rigged to the forestay, the wire that runs from the foremast to the bow.

**Forward**: at or in the direction of the bow.

**Frame (or framing)**: the structural ribs of a hull to which the planking is fastened.

**Futtock**: a curved piece of wood in a frame.

**Gaff-rigged**: a rig in which the sail has four sides. The spar to which such a sail is attached at its top is called the gaff.

**Garboard**: the lowermost plank in a hull.

**Half-breadth view (or plan)**: in the design, a view of the boat from below.

**Halyard**: a line (rope) that raises and lowers a sail.

**Hanging knee**: a structural piece that reinforces the meeting place between the deck and the hull.

**Hatch**: an opening in a deck that leads to a deck above or below.

**Heel, to**: the leaning over of a sailboat from the force of the wind.

**Horn timber**: the timber that gives structural shape and strength to the stern.

**Hull**: the body of a boat, including the deck, sides, and bottom.

**Jib**: on a two-masted schooner, the first of the four principal sails.

**Keel**: the structural backbone of a boat. Also, in a sailboat, the lowest part of the hull, which governs stability and directional control.

**Keel timber**: the principal timber to which the frames and rest of the keel are fastened.

**Kerf**: a lengthwise cut in a timber that relieves stress on the grain.

**Line**: a rope aboard a boat.

**Locker**: a small closet or storage area.

**Loft, to (and lofting)**: to transfer the lines of a hull from the drafting table and enlarge and fair them on the floor of a boatbuilding site.

**Mainmast**: on a two-masted schooner rig, the second of the two masts.

**Mainsail**: on a two-masted schooner, the last and largest sail, rigged to the mainmast.

**Marlin line**: a thin length of line, often tarred to help preserve it.

**Mast**: a tall spar along which a sail is raised and lowered.

**Mast hoop**: A wooden ring to which sails are tied and which helps them slide up and down a mast.

**Oakum**: a caulking material made of tarred yarn, hemp, or rope fibers.

**Parcel, to**: to smooth over a rigging wire by covering it with canvas or cotton.

**Pattern**: a piece of wood cut to the shape of a timber in a hull, from which the timber will be made.

**Plank (or planking)**: the outer sheathing, or covering, of the hull and deck.

**Plank-on-frame**: a type of wooden boat construction whereby planks are fastened to frames with metal and wooden fittings.

**Profile view**: in the design, a view of the boat from the side.

**Railway, marine**: a track of iron or steel on which boats are launched and hauled from the water.

**Rake**: the angle of the bow or stern as seen in profile.

**Red lead**: a primer applied to the seams after caulking, and on the bottom of a wooden boat before painting, as a preservative.

**Reefing hook**: a tool used to clean material from the seams between planks.

**Rib**: a synonym for a frame, a structural part of the hull.

**Ribbands**: lengths of wood fastened

temporarily to a hull to help hold sawn frames in place as well as guide and set steam-bent frames.

**Rig (or rigging)**: the arrangement of masts, spars, wire, and other gear on a boat. Also, to set up the wires and lines which support the masts and control the other spars.

**Saloon**: the main cabin or general living space in a boat.

**Schooner**: a sailing vessel with two or more masts, the sails usually rigged fore-and-aft (along the centerline of the boat). "Schooner" may be a derivation of an old New England word: to "scoon" or move speedily.

**Scupper**: a drain cut into the bulwark (a solid rail) around the deck.

**Seize, to**: to wrap an eye splice (or loop) of wire to help relieve tension on the splice.

**Serve, to**: to bind the outer covering the rigging tightly for further protection from wind and weather.

**Sheer (and sheerline)**: the upward sweep of a vessel's deck from the middle of the boat to the bow and the stern.

**Sheer clamp**: the interior timbers that reinforce the frames where the side of the hull meets the deck.

**Sheer plank**: the uppermost plank in a hull.

**Sheet**: a line that controls the position of a sail.

**Shroud**: one of the sets of wires that support a mast from the sides of the boat.

**Spar**: a general term for a mast or other parts of a boat to which the sails and rigging are attached.

**Spar table**: a table to which a spar, such as a mast or boom, may be clamped during its construction.

**Square-rig**: a sail rigged across a boat, so that the rig is at right-angle, or square, to the centerline of the hull; a boat so rigged is a square-rigger.

**Stay**: a wire that supports a mast from the bow or stern of a boat.

**Stave**: a length of wood, fastened together in sets, used to build a hollow mast.

**Stay**: a wire that supports a mast from the bow and stern.

**Steam-bent frame**: a timber heated in a steam box and bent into a hull to serve as a structural rib.

**Steam box**: a long box, fueled and heated in which a frame is heated so that it may be bent into a hull.

**Stem**: the most forward timber or part of the bow.

**Step, mast (and step, to)**: the foundation on which the base of a mast rests. Also the act of raising and setting a mast on a boat.

**Sternpost**: the rearmost vertical member in the framing of a boat.

**Stiffness**: the ability of a sailboat, through the design and placement of weight, to respond to the forces of various strengths of wind and waves.

**Topsail schooner**: a schooner-rigged vessel that carries square-rigged sails on the foremast.

**Transom**: the face of the boat at the stern.

**Trunnel (or tree nail)**: in traditional boat building, a wooden nail used in certain structural parts of the hull.

**Waterline**: the line along the side of a vessel indicating where the water ought to be if the vessel is floating as designed.

**Worm, to**: to fill the gaps between the strands of rigging wire with line to smooth the surface.

# *acknowledgments and thanks*

The idea, in the spring of 1996, was a simple one: In photographs and text, follow the building of a wooden boat from drawings to launch at the Gannon and Benjamin Marine Railway in Vineyard Haven. We'd taken pictures and written newspaper stories about the boatyard almost since its founding in 1980. All we needed was for the right traditional boatbuilding project to come along. How hard could it be?

Well, it took two years for *Rebecca*, a landmark schooner for Gannon and Benjamin, to get under way, another three and a half for her to move from lofting to launch, and nine more for the book to reach the date of publication. More than fourteen years when you add it up – but we knew that *Rebecca* could wait for her story to appear, however long that took.

We owe our thanks, first and last, to Nat Benjamin, Ross Gannon, and the crews of both boatbuilding sheds for welcoming our cameras, tape recorders, and us into their world. We will always be grateful that Nat and Ross entrusted us to tell the story of *Rebecca*.

SUE DAWSON

We thank Pamela and Brian Malcolm, who kindly allowed us to chronicle the construction of *Rebecca*, and Peter Normandin (a creditor in charge of the project during construction) for his support during the project. We're also grateful to Bill Graham, who commissioned Alison to photograph the construction of his gaff sloop *Maybe Baby* in 1995, which inspired this project.

Our gratitude to Jan Pogue and the late John Walter, the founding editors and publishers of Vineyard Stories, is profound. Both Jan and John wanted to publish this book from the moment they first heard of it, which cheered us six years after *Rebecca*'s launch. As editor and publisher, Jan took on a project whose photographs were already shot and notes already taken; she animated and clarified our purpose and skillfully drew from us the visual and narrative story whose possibilities had so excited us more than a decade earlier. Most of all, we're honored that Vineyard Stories has chosen to publish this, our second book, just one year after our first, *Morning Glory Farm and the Family that Feeds an Island*.

We also thank Sue Dawson, whose vision for this book helped shape it from the beginning. Her design gracefully yet energetically blends the artistic and journalistic stories of the building of *Rebecca of Vineyard Haven*. The structure, liveliness, and beauty of her layout reflects what happened at Mugwump in every way, though the story came to her only through the pictures she saw and the words she read. It takes a broad and incisive talent to make a compelling whole of such disparate parts, and there was never any other person for this job but Sue.

As we look back on our pictures and notes, we recall many people who offered us encouragement and help. Their goodwill fortified us at moments when we weren't altogether sure there would be a boat at the end of this saga, let alone a book:

Some who helped with research and technical assistance may have since forgotten the help they provided, but we have not: Mark Alan Lovewell, Eulalie Regan and Cynthia Meisner of the *Vineyard Gazette*; Peter Van Tassel and Keith Gorman at the library of the Martha's Vineyard Museum; James H. K. Norton on the history of Vineyard Haven; Ginny Jones, Kirsten Scott, and David Pritchard, who lent useful books on maritime history and boatbuilding; Claire Cain at the Alison Shaw Gallery; Carol Gannon Salguero and Sheena Bellingham at Gannon and Benjamin; Kerry E. Robinson, proprietor of the Wickford Cove Framing Gallery in Wickford, Rhode Island; Bill McConnell, and Rachel Orr.

Important elements of *Rebecca* were designed and built up and down the eastern seaboard and in the Pacific Northwest. On our travels to see ballast keels poured, masts glued up, and sails built we stayed at the homes of Pat and Alan Symonds, Glenny and Brent Bartram, Diane Abshire, and Antonio Salguero. We also received help with travel arrangements from Jackie and Paul Ronan.

Along the way, savvy and caring friends read outlines, offered support and counsel, and advocated for the book when opportunities arose: Dana Anderson, Michael F. Bamberger, Dawn Braasch of Bunch of Grapes Bookstore, Courtney S. Brady, Eric Brown of Franklin Weinrib Rudell and Vassallo P.C., the late Jim Bryan, Carol Carrick, Christopher Carrick, Elizabeth Hess, Peter Kelly, Elaine Lembo, Bellina Logan, D. Corcoran Mellon, Susan Mercier and Ann and David LeBreton of Edgartown Books, Brian Murphy, Ann Nelson, Joe Pitt, Marilyn Scheerbaum, Paul Schneider, Gail See, Blair Singer, Jamie Stringfellow, Andrew Weems, and Gwen Wynne.

Fair winds and following seas to them all, with gratitude after our own long journey.

*Alison Shaw*
*Tom Dunlop*

Most of the research for this book was conducted through interviews with those working on the *Rebecca* project at the Mugwump shed and the main Gannon and Benjamin boatyard in Vineyard Haven. In addition to those quoted here, the author interviewed the late Bill Boggess, Kerry Elkin, Henri Haukilahti, Brad Ives, Mark Laplume, and Forrest Williams.

The author also interviewed Dan Adams, Simmy Denhart, Tom Grew, Phil Hale, Tony Higgins, Caitlin Jones, Bernie Holzer, Fred Murphy, Carol Gannon Salguero, Matthew Stackpole, Victoria Street, and Jill Walsh.

Others providing insights into the history, design, and sailing characteristics of the schooner rig included Captain Robert S. Douglas of the topsail schooner *Shenandoah* of Vineyard Haven; Captain James Lobdell of the schooner *Malabar II* of Vineyard Haven; and Captain George Moffett of the schooner *Brilliant* at Mystic Seaport.

At North Sails in Stevensville, Maryland, in addition to those quoted, the author interviewed Chris Smigo, the production manager. At I. Broomfield and Sons in Providence, Rhode Island, he interviewed Tom Pratte, the foreman.

BOOKS

Blackburn, Graham. *The Overlook Illustrated Dictionary of Nautical Terms*. Woodstock, NY: The Overlook Press, 1981.

Camfield, Thomas W. *Port Townsend: An Illustrated History of Shanghaiing, Shipwrecks, Soiled Doves, and Sundry Souls*. Port Townsend, WA: Ah Tom Publishing, 2000.

Chappelle, Howard I. *Boatbuilding: A Complete Handbook of Wooden Boat Construction*. New York: Norton, 1969.

– – –, with illustrations by the author, George C. Wales, and Henry Rusk. *The History of American Sailing Ships*. New York: Bonanza Books, 1935.

Culler, Robert D. *Skiffs and Schooners*. Camden, ME: International Marine Publishing Co., 1974.

de Kerchove, René. *International Maritime Dictionary*. New York: Van Nostrand Reinhold Co. 1961.

Howland, Waldo. *Life in Boats: The Concordia Years*. Mystic, CT: Mystic Seaport Museum, 1988.

– – –. *Life in Boats: The Years before the War*. Mystic, CT: Mystic Seaport Museum, 1984.

Knox-Johnson, Robin. *Yachting: The History of a Passion*. New York: Morrow, 1990.

Macintosh, David C. "Bud," illus. by Samuel F. Manning. *How to Build a Wooden Boat*. Brooklin, ME: WoodenBoat Publications, 1987.

Norton, James H.K., with photographs by James G. Stevens. *Walking in Vineyard Haven, Massachusetts*. Edgartown, MA: Martha's Vineyard Historical Society, 2000.

Rogers, John G. *Origins of Sea Terms*. Mystic, CT: Mystic Seaport Museum, 1985.

NEWSPAPERS, MAGAZINES, PERIODICALS, BOOKLETS

*Cape Cod Canal: Interesting Facts for Navigators*
*The Christian Science Monitor*
*The Dukes County Intelligencer*
*Martha's Vineyard Magazine*
*The Martha's Vineyard Times*
*Port Townsend Leader*
*Understory: Sustainable Developments from the World of Wood*
*Vineyard Gazette*
*WoodenBoat*

WEB SITES

PT Guide, City Guide of Port Townsend. "Port Townsend History," http://www.ptguide.com/history/index.html.

U.S.C.G. Lightship Sailors Association International, Inc. History of Cross Rip Lightship No. 5, 1867–1915, http://www.uscglightshipsailors.org/cross_rip_lightship_lv5.htm.

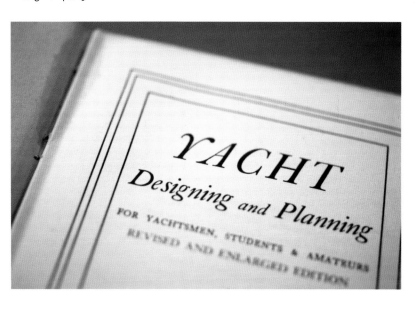

# the end

Ross Gannon's young son, Olin,
in a moment of blissful abandon
aboard *Rebecca*.